C000064896

JANE AUSTEN

AMAZING AND EXTRAORDINARY FACTS

JANE AUSTEN

Henrietta Heald

RP

RYDON
PUBLISHING

A Rydon Publishing Book
35 The Quadrant
Hassocks
West Sussex
BN6 8BP
www.rydonpublishing.co.uk
www.rydonpublishing.com

First published by Rydon Publishing in 2016

A CIP catalogue record for this book is available from the British Library.

ISBN: 978-1-910821-12-1

Printed in Poland by BZ Graf S.A.

CONTENTS

INTRODUCTION

When I began research for this book, I did not know much about Jane Austen's life. I had loved her novels since schooldays, and come to appreciate them more as I grew older, but I had a limited vision of her as a person. I suppose I imagined Jane sitting by the fire in her father's rectory, writing letters, doing embroidery, or genteelly pouring tea into bone-china cups. She did all these things, of course – and so much more.

It strikes me now that Steventon Rectory, her childhood home, must have been an endlessly stimulating place to grow up. Ordinary family tensions apart, the Austen household was often full of joy and laughter. The Austens were a close band who rallied when problems arose. They read stories to each other, acted together, played games together – and, when death took one of their extended family or circle of friends, they mourned together.

Jane's seven siblings – James, George, Edward, Henry, Cassandra, Francis (Frank) and Charles – were all intriguing individuals, although George had a strange illness that isolated him from the rest. Both Frank and Charles went into the navy aged 12 and both rose to the rank of admiral. Edward was adopted by a rich, childless couple and inherited their wealth, rescuing his mother and sisters at a time of financial crisis. James and Henry led more conventional lives, though Henry changed career several times. Together with their friends among the gentry and aristocracy, the Austen family provided Jane with a rich source of material for her fiction.

The author's letters to her sister, Cassandra, reveal much about her literary exploits and her opinions of others, although her emotional life remains mysterious. Both sisters were childless, and there is no doubt that, for Jane, her books took the place of children. She also showed a great interest in her many nephews and nieces, and corresponded with those who sought her advice. One of her nephews, Edward Austen-Leigh, wrote a detailed memoir of his aunt, published in 1870, which has formed the starting point for all the biographical works that followed.

Like the reader of her fiction, the student of Jane Austen's life instinctively wants the heroine to get her man and, ideally, to live happily ever afterwards – so it is upsetting at first to learn that she refused the only man who proposed to her. On reflection, however, it is clear that, had Jane Austen been required to fulfil the duties of a wife and mother, she could never have achieved literary greatness. Seen in this light, her dramatic rejection of Harris Bigg-Wither represents a moment of enlightenment about her own destiny. Her decision not to marry paved the way for the move to Chawton cottage, where she wrote or revised for publication her six completed novels.

The contrast between Jane's life at Steventon and the final eight years at Chawton is striking. Apart from attending to domestic duties, she spent most of her time at Chawton writing. Her social intercourse during this period was very limited. It was as if the first part of her life had been devoted to gathering material, and the second part to transforming that material into matchless works of art.

Jane Austen was an outstanding writer whose genius continues to be appreciated all over the world, but she could never have imagined becoming the cult figure she is today. Her life and works are fascinating subjects of study, but part of the fun of writing this book has been the discovery of amazing and extraordinary facts pertaining to modern Austen worship in the form of blogs, websites, festivals, fan clubs, literary imitators, and devotees of Regency food and fashion – to say nothing of more than 50 screen adaptations of her work, including portrayals of Mr Darcy by everyone from Laurence Olivier to a dog named Wishbone.

Henrietta Heald

Class act
George and Cassandra Austen

Social class – and the tensions it can cause – played a part in Jane Austen's life even before her birth in 1775, since her parents, George and Cassandra, came from markedly different backgrounds. Despite the contrast in their social standing, however, the Austens had a strong marriage and brought up their eight children in a secure and loving home.

George Austen (1731–1805) was described by his son Henry as 'a profound scholar' who possessed 'a most exquisite taste in every species of literature'. Henry said that, with such a father, it was no surprise that 'Jane should, at a very early age, have become sensible to the charms of style, and enthusiastic in the cultivation of her own language.'

In childhood, George had not seemed destined for a distinguished career. His own parents were William Austen, a lowly surgeon from Tonbridge in Kent, and Rebecca née Hampson – who, at the time of her marriage to Austen, was Rebecca Walter, a widow with one son.

Orphaned at the age of six, George was lucky enough to have a wealthy uncle, Francis Austen, who helped him to get on in life. He attended Tonbridge School, followed by St John's College, Oxford, where he was awarded a scholarship. George was made a Fellow of St John's in 1759 and took holy orders soon afterwards, and in 1764 he married Cassandra Leigh at Walcot Church in Bath. His bright hazel eyes and curly white hair had won him the nickname of 'the handsome proctor'.

Although the new Mrs Austen was not rich, she had aristocratic pretensions and elevated social connections. An ancestor, Sir Thomas Leigh, had been Lord Mayor of London during the reign of Queen Elizabeth I. In 1642, his son had sheltered King Charles I at Stoneleigh Abbey in Warwickshire, the seat of the Leighs of Adlestrop, Cassandra's branch of the family (see Opulent Magnificence).

Cassandra, like George, was clever and good-looking, with an

Stoneleigh Abbey in Warwickshire

aquiline nose that, she believed, gave her a superior demeanour. She had a robust sense of humour and wrote amusing light verse, as well as captivating family and friends with her witty conversation.

Both parents exerted a strong, if unconscious, influence on Jane Austen as a writer. From her father she acquired a love of literature and a feeling for literary style; from her mother she gained an appreciation of the comedy inherent in human relationships and the power of shrewd judgement.

BUMPY RIDE

After Jane Austen's father, George, took on the living of the church of St Nicholas at Steventon near Basingstoke in 1764, he and his new wife, Cassandra, lived at first in the nearby village of Deane while improvements were made to Steventon Rectory. When the Austens eventually moved from Deane to Steventon in 1771, the road was 'a mere cart track, so cut up by deep ruts as to be impassable for a light carriage', according to Edward Austen-Leigh, their grandson. In the event, Mrs Austen, who was not in good health at the time, was obliged to '[perform] the journey on a feather-bed, placed upon some soft articles of furniture in the waggon which held their household goods'.

'Bad reckoners'
Jane Austen's birth is announced

Although some correspondence about important events in Jane Austen's life has been lost, an amusing letter giving details of her birth has survived – amusing on account of its reference to her parents as 'bad reckoners'. By the time of Jane's birth on 16 December 1775, her parents, George and Cassandra, already had six children, so they might have been expected to make a more accurate guess at their new baby's date of birth than proved to be the case.

On 17 December 1775, Rev. George Austen wrote from the family home at Steventon Rectory, Hampshire, to his sister-in-law Susanna Walter (the wife of his half-brother, William Hampson Walter), announcing the apparently trouble-free birth and remarking on the new arrival's physical likeness to her brother Henry:

Dear Sister

You have doubtless been for some time in expectation of hearing from Hampshire, and perhaps wondered a little we were in our old age grown such bad reckoners, but so it was, for Cassy certainly expected to have been brought to bed a month ago; however, last night the time came and without a great deal of warning, everything was soon happily over. We have now another girl, a present plaything for her sister Cassy and a future companion. She is to be Jenny, and seems to me as if she would be as like Henry, as Cassy is to Neddy. Your sister, thank God, is pure well after it and sends her love to you and my brother, not forgetting James and Philly…

I am, dear Sister,
Your affecte. brother
Geo. Austen

During their period at Deane Rectory, George and Cassandra Austen had been blessed with three sons: James (1765), George

(1766) and Edward (1767). After they moved to Steventon Rectory a few years later, they had five more children: Henry (1771), Cassandra (1773), Francis (1774), Jane (1775) and Charles (1779).

DISPATCHED 'TO NURSE'

For the first year or so of their lives, the Austen children were sent away from Steventon Rectory 'to nurse' – that is, to be breastfed by a wet nurse – in neighbouring villages. This, it seems, was not unusual at the time and no neglect was implied by it. They were visited constantly by their parents, as was confirmed in letters between Mrs Austen and her sister-in-law Mrs Walter. When her elder daughter, Cassandra, returned home from her nurse, Mrs Austen wrote to Susanna Walter to tell her of an apparent new discovery about her daughter: 'My little girl talks all day long, and, in my opinion, is a very entertaining companion.'

Jane Austen was the seventh child of eight

112-year association
The Austen family's long tenure at Steventon

Jane Austen's father, George, acquired the living of the church of St Nicholas at Steventon in 1761 and held it for almost 40 years, until his retirement in 1800. George was followed as rector by, in succession, his sons James and Henry then his grandson William Knight. William ministered there for 50 years, until his death in 1878 finally ended the 112-year association between Steventon church and the Austen family.

Standing apart from the village on an upland site 7 miles (11km) west of Basingstoke, Steventon church has changed little from when it was built by the lord of the manor in the 12th century. It was constructed of Binstead limestone from the Isle of Wight – the same stone used to build Winchester Cathedral, Chichester Cathedral and part of the Tower of London. Predating the church is a Saxon cross, apparently from the 9th century, indicating that Steventon was an ancient holy site.

There are several memorials in the church to the Austens and the Digweeds, the tenant farmers who lived in Steventon Manor from the mid-18th century. Most poignant of these is a memorial to the Rev. William Knight's three daughters, Mary Agnes, Cecilia and Augusta, all of whom died of scarlet fever in a single week in 1848 at the ages of five, four and three.

Some of Jane Austen's relations lie buried in the churchyard, in particular her eldest brother, James, and his two wives, Anne (née Mathew) and Mary (née Lloyd).

Jane Leigh, the novelist's maternal grandmother, is buried in a vault under the chancel. There is a bronze plaque in the church dedicated to Jane Austen, and another plaque recognizes the support of the Jane Austen Society of North America, which paid for the refurbishment of the church bells in January 1995.

Church of St Nicholas at Steventon

Happy home
But Steventon Rectory finally destroyed by floods

Located at the bottom of Steventon hill at one end of a street of cottages, and on a site vulnerable to flooding, Steventon Rectory was the home of the Austen family for many years and consisted of a two-storey building with dormer attic windows. It stood about half a mile from the church in 2½ acres of land which encompassed stables and other outbuildings, including a large barn that played an important part in family entertainments.

George Austen added an extension to the southwest side of the house. It was designed so that his bow-windowed study would look over the garden, which was backed by a thatched wall and shadowed by a row of elms. The inside of the house was plain and sparsely furnished because, although well off by country clergyman's standards, George Austen could not afford luxuries. In the garden was a turfed slope down which the young Jane Austen – like Catherine Morland in *Northanger Abbey* – was fond of rolling. It was in this house that Jane composed her first three novels, destined to become *Sense and Sensibility*, *Pride and Prejudice* and *Northanger Abbey*, although originally all had different names.

The Austen rectory had three living rooms, seven bedrooms and three attics. In addition to accommodating his many children, who came and went at intervals, George took in a series of live-in students to supplement the family income. His daughters, Cassandra and Jane, had been sent away to school at the ages of nine and seven, but their experiences of formal schooling were less than happy and in 1787 the girls returned to Steventon to be educated at home. From here the sisters maintained a wide circle of friends among the local gentry and aristocracy (see Good Friends); they called on their friends regularly and attended their balls. Cassandra and Jane continued to enjoy life at Steventon to the full until their father's retirement in 1801, after which the family moved to Bath (see 'It's All Settled!').

The old rectory was pulled down in 1826, following a serious flood six years earlier that had made the ground floor uninhabitable. The flood had occurred soon after the installation as rector of William Knight, son of Jane's brother Edward (who had changed his surname to Knight in recognition of his large inheritance from the Knight family). Edward Knight decided to build his son a new home set in 20 acres of parkland on the hill opposite, which was completed in 1825.

In later years, William Knight was blamed for knocking down the old cottages in the valley because they spoilt the view from his new house, but he was not in fact responsible for this. Two of the cottages had caught fire in March 1808; others had fallen into disrepair and been demolished; and the flood of January 1820 probably made the remainder inhabitable.

The new hilltop site suited William Knight and his family – although he and his wife would suffer a tragedy there in 1848, when all three of their young daughters died of scarlet fever. The 1825 rectory had grander drawing and dining rooms than its predecessor, five main bedrooms, a bathroom and four attic bedrooms, not counting the three maids'

Steventon Rectory in 1871

bedrooms, the kitchen and a servants' hall. William lived there until his death in 1878.

THE GRATITUDE OF HASTINGS

George Austen, Jane's father, had a sister called Philadelphia. In 1752 she travelled to India, where she married Dr Tysoe Hancock and befriended the wife of the colonial administrator Warren Hastings. In 1759 Mrs Hastings died in childbirth, leaving a three-year-old son, who was sent to England to be looked after by George Austen and his wife. Sadly, the boy expired at the age of six from 'a putrid sore throat' – a common ailment at the time. But out of gratitude to the Austens and the Hancocks for their care of his son, Warren Hastings set up a trust fund in the name of Philadelphia's daughter, Eliza, and endowed it with £10,000. Eliza, who later became the Comtesse de Feuillide (see Leading Lady), gave the name of Hastings to her baby son, born in 1797.

Warren Hastings

Three grand houses
The tale of Steventon Manor

A short distance away from Steventon's church of St Nicholas, which was closely associated with the Austen family for more than a century, stands Steventon Manor. In 1877 Henry Harris, a prosperous corn merchant, bought the 2,000-acre Steventon estate from the 2nd Duke of Wellington and commissioned the celebrated architect Alfred

Waterhouse to design him a Gothic Revival mansion on the hill next to the Norman church. Better known as the architect of Manchester Town Hall and the Natural History Museum in London, Waterhouse designed Steventon Manor on a grand scale, with four great reception rooms and 22 bedrooms.

However, the hill at Steventon was no stranger to grand residences – for Waterhouse's mansion was the third substantial manor house to be located there. The first such edifice was a 12th-century Norman stronghold built in a square, parts of which survived into the 19th century as farm buildings. This was superseded in Elizabethan times by an elegant manor with tall patterned chimneys and stone-mullioned windows. This had been begun by Sir Richard Pexall, but by the time of Pexall's death in 1571 only one wing had been completed – and no major additions were made for three centuries.

It was the Tudor manor, therefore, that Jane Austen and her family knew well during their time at Steventon

Rectory (see Happy Home), in the valley below. At that period, the house was tenanted by a family of gentlemen farmers, the Digweeds, who were very close to the Austens. Indeed, there was an occasional hint of romance between the two families, with Jane once writing to her sister, Cassandra, that James Digweed 'must be in love with you'.

In 1932, most of the Victorian mansion built on Steventon hill by Henry Harris and Alfred Waterhouse was destroyed in a great fire, but it has since been restored on a more modest scale.

Second Farmer George
George Austen embraces the Agricultural Revolution

Rev. George Austen, Jane's father, is remembered primarily as a bookish man and an affectionate father who played a crucial role in his children's education, but there was another side to him that revealed itself in his enthusiasm for innovative farming methods. This interest reflected the revolution under way in British agricultural practices, which gathered pace in the mid-18th century, particularly concerning crop rotation and better livestock husbandry. The new methods were keenly supported by King George III, who admired a form of land management that '[united] the system of continued pasture with cultivation'. The king's passion for agriculture earned him the nickname Farmer George, and he would later create three model farms on his estate at Windsor.

When not absorbed in his duties as a minister of the church, George Austen was himself preoccupied by improving the productivity of his 200 acres of farmland at Steventon. In this he was pursuing a tradition already well established in the village, for when the estate of Steventon Manor was indentured in 1758 to the Richard Digweeds, father and son, its owner specified in the lease how the estate should be farmed to ensure its fertility and productiveness. Wheat was the main crop, and the owner was keen that the wheatfields should be fallowed and manured to preserve their fertility. There were

King George III

meadows for sheep and pasture for cows and horses.

Thirty years later, George Austen was actively engaged in improving his own land, probably producing wheat, peas and barley undersown with clover in rotation, increasing yields and rental values – and making him better able to support his growing family. Indeed, although it was achieved on a small scale, George Austen's contribution to agriculture should have made him a candidate for the title of 'a second Farmer George'.

SCHOLARS AT STEVENTON

From the early 1770s, George Austen started taking resident pupils at Steventon Rectory to supplement his income as a country parson. Among these was Viscount Lymington, the son of the Earl of Portsmouth, who arrived at the age of six; he would later invite the Austen girls to balls at Hurstbourne Park, the family seat. Another pupil was Thomas Craven Fowle, who in 1795 became engaged to Jane's sister, Cassandra. The Austens had earlier taken charge of George Hastings, the motherless three-year-old son of Warren Hastings, the future Governor-General of India (see The Gratitude of Hastings). Mrs Austen appears to have been deeply involved in the school at Steventon Rectory, looking after the pupils as if they were part of her extended family.

School pupil in the 18th century

The Loiterer
James Austen edits satirical review

Jane Austen found her brother James increasingly tiresome as he grew older, especially after his second marriage to her erstwhile friend, Mary Lloyd. But during their childhood he was an important influence on her incipient literary career, writing poems and stories, and taking on the role of dramatist in the home theatricals that were so popular in the Austen household.

James was the eldest son of George and Cassandra Austen's eight children. According to his mother, he possessed 'classical knowledge, literary taste, and the power of elegant composition…in the highest degree'. His intellectual skills were evident from early in life and he went up to Oxford University in 1779, at the age of just 14.

At Oxford, James attended his father's old college, St John's, but in the capacity of 'Founder's Kin', through connections of his mother, who was born Cassandra Leigh (see Class Act). Among other Oxford luminaries of the time was his mother's formidable uncle, Theophilus Leigh, who was Master of Balliol College for the record term of 59 years, from 1726 to 1785.

James Austen took pleasure in parodying the behaviour of the typically idle and over-privileged Oxford 'swell', whose life seemed to consist mostly of hunting, eating, drinking and gambling. For this purpose, he set up with his brother Henry, who was also at Oxford, a university magazine called *The Loiterer* that ran for 60 issues, with James as both the editor and the principal contributor.

The Loiterer of 21 February 1789 included a weekly 'Diary of a Modern Oxford Man'. Apparently written after a day of falls in the hunting field, the entry for Tuesday ran as follows:

> Very bruised and sore, did not get up till twelve – found an imposition on my table – mem. to give it to the hairdresser – drank six dishes of tea – did not know what to do with myself, so wrote to my father for money. – Half after one, put on my boots to ride for an hour – met Careless at the stable – rode together – asked me to dine with him and meet Jack Sedley, who is just returned from France – two to three, returned home and dressed – four to seven, dinner and wine – Jack very pleasant – told some good stories – says the French women have thick legs – no hunting to be got, and very

James Austen

him. – Drank a little punch, and went to bed at twelve.

In 1787, James Austen was ordained as a clergyman and later succeeded his father as rector of Steventon (see 112-Year Association). He married twice, first to Anna Mathew, who died in 1795, two years after the birth of their daughter, Anna, and then to Mary Lloyd, by whom he had a son and a daughter, James Edward and Caroline.

little wine – won't go there in a hurry – seven, went to the stable and then looked in at the coffee-house – very few drunken men, and nothing going forwards – agreed to play Sedley at Billiards – Walker's table engaged, and forced to go to the Blue Posts – lost two guineas – thought I could have beat him, but the dog has been practising in France – ten, supper at Careless's – bought Sedley's mare for thirty guineas – think he knows nothing of a horse, and believe I have done

Chosen as heir
Edward Austen is adopted by the Knights

George Austen owed what financial security he had to the generosity of family relations, in particular Thomas Knight, who owned hundreds of acres of land in Kent – centred on his country seat, Godmersham Park – and in Hampshire, including Chawton Manor House near Alton. The living of Steventon, off the Basingstoke to Andover road, was in his gift, and in 1761 he had presented this to his relatively poor second cousin George Austen, who had recently taken holy orders. (George's uncle Francis Austen, who had acted as guardian to his nephew since the boy was orphaned in childhood, subsequently bought the livings of two nearby parishes, Deane and Ashe, intending to give George which ever fell vacant first.)

George Austen's main benefactor had a son, also Thomas, who was childless as well as rich. Thomas Knight the younger and his wife Catherine grew very fond of George's son, Edward Austen (born 1767), who often visited them in Kent. Edward's frequent absences did not go down well with George, who complained that his son was falling behind with his Latin studies, but he deferred to Cassandra when she said, 'You had better oblige your cousins and let him go.'

Surprising as it may seem, when the Knights asked to adopt Edward and bring him up as their heir at Godmersham Park, the Austens

Godmersham Park in Kent

agreed – presumably thinking it would give him advantages that were not available to their other offspring. Described by his mother as 'quite a man of business', Edward was by all accounts practical and sensible, making him a good choice to run the Knight estates in later life. He was sent by his adoptive parents on the Grand Tour of Europe in 1786–88, and in 1791 he married Elizabeth Bridges, with whom he had 11 children before her death in 1808.

In 1797 Edward Austen reaped the full benefits of being adopted by the Knights. Thomas Knight had died in 1794, leaving his fortune and estates to his wife. Three years later, Mrs Knight passed on Godmersham to Edward, along with the property and lands at Chawton and most of the family wealth. She moved to a small house, White Friars near Canterbury, and retained only £2,000 a year for herself. Edward could now entertain his parents, sisters and brothers in

George Austen presenting his son Edward to Mr and Mrs Thomas Knight

a magnificent neoclassical mansion where the luxurious style of life was in marked contrast to the simplicity they were used to.

Fifteen years later, in 1812, Edward took the surname Knight.

FAMILY MYSTERY

One unexplained mystery surrounds the Austen family. The second son, George, who was born in 1766, lived most of his life with another family in Monks Sherborne, about 12 miles (19km) from Steventon, and it is known that money was paid for his keep. A letter written by Mrs Austen in 1770 tells of 'poor little George' being brought to see her, and her hope that he might have no more fits. Apart from this, no reference to him appears in family letters or memoirs, except for an announcement of his death in 1838. Jane Austen's ability to make herself understood using sign language has been cited as evidence that George was a deaf mute. However it is perhaps more likely that he suffered from some form of long-term illness that carried a stigma, such as epilepsy.

Juvenile parody
Jane Austen writes a history of England

In 1791, when Jane Austen was barely 16 years old, she set out to write a history of England. Needless to say, this was not meant to be a very serious or learned account. These are the words on the title page:

> *The History of England*
> *from the reign of Henry the 4th*
> *to the death of Charles the 1st*

> *By a partial, prejudiced, and ignorant Historian*

> *To Miss Austen, eldest daughter of the Rev. George Austen, this work is inscribed with all due respect by The Author*

> *N.B. There will be very few Dates in this History.*

In fact, Jane was parodying a monumental tome that she and her siblings had been obliged to read regularly as part of their home studies. This was Oliver Goldsmith's four-volume *The History of England from the Earliest Times to the Death of George II.* The Austen family's copy of this book is full of scribbled notes and criticisms in the margins, for they apparently shared the view of history expressed by 17-year-old Catherine Morland in *Northanger Abbey*, revealed during a conversation with Mr and Miss Tilney: 'History, real solemn history, I cannot be interested in… I read it a little as a duty, but it tells me nothing that does not either vex or weary me. The quarrels of popes or kings, with wars and pestilences, in every page; the men all so good for nothing, and hardly any women at all.'

Jane Austen's historical parody was among 26 items of juvenilia, written between 1787 and 1793, which she later made into a 'collected edition'. She copied them into three notebooks that she entitled *Volume the First*, *Volume the Second* and *Volume the Third*. 'The History of England', which appears in *Volume the Second*, includes irreverent sketches by her sister,

Cassandra, portraying the monarchs not as grandly dressed heads of state but rather as unsophisticated ordinary folk.

Jane Austen's account prefigures the wildly popular spoof *1066 And All That* (1930) by W. C. Sellar and R. J. Yeatman, who subtitled their work 'A memorable history of England, comprising all the parts you can remember including 103 good things, 5 bad kings, and 2 genuine dates.' Like Jane's earlier account, *1066 And All That* is full of examples of half-recalled and distorted facts, reflecting the authors' assertion that: 'History is not what you thought. It is what you can remember.'

Jane's history also includes a great deal of authorial opinion and fantasy about what might have been, sometimes involving friends and family members. One person to feature in the section on Queen Elizabeth I is Jane's brother Francis (Frank), then aged 17 and serving as a midshipman aboard HMS *Perseverance*. He is mentioned in the same breath as Sir Francis Drake, 'the first English Navigator who sailed round the World'. Jane goes on to write:

> Yet great as [Drake] was, & justly celebrated as a Sailor, I cannot help foreseeing that he will be equalled in this or the next Century by one who tho' now but young, already promises to answer all the ardent and sanguine expectations of his Relations & Friends, amongst whom I may class the amiable Lady to whom this work is dedicated [Cassandra], & my no less amiable Self.

After Jane Austen's death, Cassandra kept the three notebooks until her own death in 1845. Then she bequeathed *Volume the First* to her youngest brother Charles, *Volume the Third* to her nephew James Edward, and *Volume the Second* to their brother Frank.

Jane and Cassandra
A lifelong attachment between sisters

The correspondence between Jane Austen and her only sister, Cassandra, is a rich source of information about the novelist's personal and family life. The surviving letters, almost all of which are written to Cassandra from Jane, start in January 1796. Since they were written when the sisters were apart, they offer only a partial picture of Jane's life – especially since, after Jane's death, Cassandra decided to edit or destroy the most sensitive material. Nevertheless, they reflect a lifelong bond of affection between the two women, a bond that was forged in early childhood.

In 1782 Cassandra and Jane Austen, aged 9 and 7, were sent away from home to Oxford for schooling by a Mrs Cawley, the widow of a principal of Brasenose College. At first, Jane had been thought too young to be sent away from home, but Mrs Austen's decision was influenced by the extraordinarily close relationship between her two daughters. 'If Cassandra were going to have her head cut off, Jane would insist on sharing her fate,' she once said.

The following year Mrs Cawley's school moved to Southampton. After an outbreak of 'putrid sore throat', the Austen sisters and their cousin Jane Cooper were taken away and sent instead to the Abbey School in Reading, located in the gatehouse of the old abbey. Even though this establishment seems to have been altogether more satisfactory than Mrs Cawley's, the girls' formal education there did not last long. By 1787 they were back in Steventon and immersed in home schooling. Their father was a classical scholar with an excellent

The gatehouse at Reading Abbey

library, and no restriction seems to have been put on the girls' reading or conversation.

The attachment between the two sisters was never interrupted or weakened, according to their nephew Edward Austen-Leigh in his memoir of Jane Austen. 'They lived in the same home, and shared the same bedroom, till separated by death,' he wrote, also commenting that they were not exactly alike. 'Cassandra's was the colder and calmer disposition; she was always prudent and well judging, but with less outward demonstration of feeling and less sunniness of temper than Jane possessed.'

Cassandra's love affair with Thomas Fowle, a former pupil of her father, ended in tragedy when he died on an expedition to the West Indies, and she never married (see Death in the Caribbean). In July 1809, she and Jane, along with their mother and good friend Martha Lloyd, moved into the Chawton cottage that had been provided for them by their brother Edward. After the death of Jane in 1817, and that of her mother a decade later, followed by the marriage of Martha Lloyd to her brother Frank, Cassandra lived alone at Chawton until her own death in 1845, aged 72. She is buried at St Nicholas Church, Chawton, alongside her mother.

MODE OF ADDRESS

Almost all Jane Austen's surviving letters are written to her only sister, Cassandra (see Jane and Cassandra), who was two years her senior. They are addressed to 'Miss Austen', the correct mode of address for the eldest unmarried daughter of a family. Cassandra's replies would have been addressed to 'Miss Jane Austen', the correct mode of address for any but the eldest daughter. Jane, like most people of her class and time, was punctilious in observing such etiquette. In **Mansfield Park** *for example, Tom Bertram, the elder son, is 'Mr Bertram' – and much is made of the fact that, were he to die, his younger brother, Mr Edmund Bertram, would become 'Mr Bertram' in his stead. The elder sister, Maria, is until her marriage always spoken of as 'Miss Bertram' and her younger sister as 'Miss Julia Bertram'.*

Good friends
Society at Steventon and beyond

In spite of its rural setting, the village of Steventon was well placed for transport links, being located just a couple of miles from the main carriage route between Oxford and Southampton (via Winchester), and almost equidistant between the two cities. It was also within relatively easy reach of both London and Bath. Its propitious geographical location in the midst of the agrarian riches of Hampshire meant that the preponderance of 'big houses' in the area was no coincidence. This gave the Austen family plenty of opportunities to mix with the local gentry and aristocracy – and this in turn gave Jane Austen plenty of source material for her novels.

Steventon Manor, which had an absentee landlord, was rented to a congenial family, the Digweeds, and nearby Deane House was occupied by the Harwoods, who gave frequent balls. Among other friends of the Austens were the Bigg-Wither family at Manydown House near Basingstoke, where Cassandra and Jane Austen would often stay after attending a ball at the assembly rooms of Basingstoke's Angel Inn.

The Austens' best friends in the immediate neighbourhood were the Lefroys and the Lloyds. They occupied, respectively, the rectories of Ashe and Deane, the two livings bought by Francis Austen (see Chosen as Heir).

When the Austens moved to Steventon in 1764, Ashe Rectory had been occupied by a Dr Russell. In 1783, Russell was succeeded by Isaac Lefroy, a former Fellow of All Souls, Oxford. His wife Anne, often referred to as Madam Lefroy, became a close confidante of Jane Austen. In 1814 the two families were linked by the marriage of Madam Lefroy's son Benjamin to Jane's niece Anna. Tom Lefroy, a cousin of the Lefroys of Ashe, had fallen in love with Jane in the mid-1790s, but their relationship was doomed because neither had money (see The Tom Lefroy Affair).

Meanwhile, the rectory at Deane was occupied by a family called Lloyd. The father had died in 1789, leaving Mrs Lloyd with three

Ibthorpe House, home of the Lloyd family

daughters, two of whom, Martha and Mary, were still living at home. In 1797 Mary married James Austen, Jane's eldest brother, after the death of his first wife, Anne Mathew, two years earlier.

In 1792 Mrs Lloyd, Martha and Mary moved to the village of Ibthorpe, 30 miles (48km) northwest of Steventon and 6 miles (10km) north of Andover, where they stayed for 13 years. Jane Austen often visited Ibthorpe and was staying there with the Lloyds when she attended her first dance as an adult at Enham House near Andover. Their home, Ibthorpe House, is mentioned in many of her letters.

Jane's sister, Cassandra, helped Martha to nurse Mrs Lloyd in her final illness. After the latter's death at Ibthorpe in April 1805, Martha moved in with the Austens at Bath and remained with them after their move to Chawton in 1809. This was an arrangement that suited everyone and Martha stayed for about 20 years. In 1828 she married Jane's brother Frank after the death of Frank's first wife, Mary, with whom he had 11 children.

Leading lady
Austens' notorious Cousin Eliza

The younger members of the Austen family at Steventon always looked forward to visits from their exotic cousin Eliza Hancock, who had been born in India and spent much of her life in France. Her parents were Dr Tysoe Hancock, a former physician with the East India Company, and George Austen's sister, Philadelphia – although there was a rumour that Eliza was the illegitimate daughter of Warren Hastings, the future Governor-General of India. Eliza was vivacious and flirtatious, particularly in the company of Jane's brother Henry, and she loved taking part in the family theatricals that were so popular with the Austen children.

Dr Hancock had brought his wife and daughter home from the colonies in 1765. He returned to India in 1769 to earn some money, dying there in 1775. But during this period Eliza and her mother remained in Europe, first in England – where they spent most of

Eliza de Feuillide

their time at Steventon, becoming effectively part of the Austen family – and then, from 1780, in Paris.

At the age of 20, Eliza married a French officer called Jean-François Capot, Comte de Feuillide, cementing her position in Parisian high society. On becoming pregnant in 1786, Eliza returned to England with her mother, intending to stay there until the baby was born. She received a warm welcome at Steventon Rectory, where she amused her

cousins with tales of life in Paris.

Eliza was at Steventon for the Christmas of 1787, following the birth of her son Hastings, and eager to take part in the family dramas. The Austens were keen amateur actors, and sometimes produced two plays in a year. For example, in 1783 they had staged performances of Sheridan's *The Rivals* and of Thomas Francklin's tragedy *Matilda*. In summer they used a barn, which had been fitted out as a theatre, to stage their plays; in winter, they used the rectory dining room. These productions were carefully planned and organized events, for which James Austen generally wrote prologues and epilogues. On this occasion, James wrote a prologue to introduce two comedies, in both of which Eliza and his brother Henry played leading roles.

Jane Austen would make use of the private theatricals of 1787 more than 20 years later in *Mansfield Park*, when the propriety of a scheme to stage a play called *Lovers' Vows* divides opinion among the assembled company – with Edmund Bertram and Fanny Price united in objecting to it. Indeed Eliza is believed to have been an inspirational element in a number of Austen's works, such as *Love and Freindship* [sic] and *Lady Susan*. She may also have been the model for the character of Mary Crawford in *Mansfield Park*.

The Austen scholar Deirdre Le Faye wrote a book based on Eliza's letters, published in 2002, entitled *Jane Austen's Outlandish Cousin, The Life and Letters of Eliza de Feuillide*. The author points out that, as well as being a highly entertaining social and historical record of the time, many of Eliza's letters vividly illuminate the lives of Jane Austen and her family.

In 1797, three years after her first husband had been guillotined during the Terror that followed the French Revolution (see 'Enemy of the Republic' Guillotined), Eliza de Feuillide married Jane Austen's favourite brother, Henry.

'ENEMY OF THE REPUBLIC' GUILLOTINED

In 1781 Jane Austen's cousin Eliza Hancock married a French officer, Jean-François Capot, Comte de Feuillide, an ardent supporter of the **ancien régime** *(see Leading Lady). 'He literally adores me,' Eliza wrote excitedly to her cousin Philadelphia Walter, but Eliza herself was apparently more in love with the glamour of Paris than with her husband. The outbreak of the French Revolution in 1789 threatened the de Feuillides' privileged existence and they retreated to England. In 1794, a year after the start of the Reign of Terror, the Comte de Feuillide, who had returned to France to save his estates, was arrested in Paris and sent to the guillotine as an enemy of the republic.*

Death in the Caribbean
Cassandra Austen's love match ends in tragedy

Cassandra Austen, Jane's sister, fell in love with Thomas Fowle, a former Oxford scholar who seemed destined for a career in the church, and in 1795 she agreed to marry him. Thomas Fowle had first met Cassandra while a pupil of her father at Steventon Rectory and had taken part in some of the Austen family's private theatrical performances.

Neither Cassandra nor Thomas had much money, but they were determined not to let this get in the way of their romantic inclinations. The engagement was welcomed by both families – partly because Thomas was the brother of Fulwar Craven Fowle, the vicar of Kintbury in Wiltshire, who had married Eliza Lloyd. (Eliza's family were the Lloyds of Deane, the neighbouring village to Steventon, and both her sisters would go on to marry Austen brothers – see Good Friends.)

Thomas's patron and cousin, Lord Craven, had promised him the living of Ryton in Shropshire. On the basis of this expectation, which would yield only a bachelor's income, the young couple decided to marry when the appointment took effect two years in the future.

In the meantime, in ignorance of the engagement, Lord Craven offered Thomas the post of chaplain to his regiment, which was going out to the West Indies. Thomas accepted the offer, reasoning that it would give him the opportunity to save money in advance of the marriage. Then tragedy struck. Thomas sailed in 1796 and while in Santo Domingo (in what is now the Dominican Republic) he contracted yellow fever, of which he died in February 1797.

Cassandra inherited £1,000 from Thomas, which gave her some financial independence, but she was devastated by his loss. Although Cassandra lived for another 48 years, dying in 1845 at the age of 72, it appears that she never again considered marriage.

ELINOR'S SENSIBILITY

Jane Austen doted on her elder sister and was profoundly affected by the death of Cassandra's suitor, Thomas Fowle (see Death in the Caribbean), and the fortitude with which she bore it. In **Jane Austen and Her Art,** *the biographer Mary Lascelles puts forward the theory that Cassandra's bereavement strongly influenced the portrayal of Elinor Dashwood in* **Sense and Sensibility.** *Referring to the grace and restraint with which Elinor endures her disappointment in love, Lascelles argues that the one occasion on which Jane Austen allowed her own life experience directly to enter a novel was in her defence of Elinor Dashwood and her insistence that strength in the face of adversity is no indication of insensitivity.*

John and Elinor Dashwood in Sense and Sensibility

The Tom Lefroy affair
A foretaste of
Pride and Prejudice

In a letter of January 1796, Jane Austen breaks the news to her sister, Cassandra, of her flirtation with Thomas Langlois Lefroy (1776–1869), a young Irish cousin of the Lefroys of Ashe, who were close friends of the Austen family (see Good Friends):

> He is a very gentlemanlike, good-looking, pleasant young man, I assure you. But as to our having ever met, except at the last three balls, I cannot say much; for he is so excessively laughed at about me at Ashe, that he is ashamed of coming to Steventon, and ran away when we called on Mrs Lefroy a few days ago.

Tom Lefroy's relationship with Jane Austen could come to nothing and everyone realized it. The reason was money – or the lack of it. Tom was keen to pursue a career in the legal profession, but he had no financial means. Jane had no means either, and Tom, if he were to fulfil his ambitions, would have to acquire money through marriage.

Despite this obstacle, the young couple were open about their affection for each other. When mildly criticized by Cassandra, Jane was far from bashful about her flirtation with Tom:

> You scold me so much in the nice long letter which I have this moment received from you, that I am almost afraid to tell you how my Irish friend and I behaved. Imagine to yourself everything most profligate and shocking in the way of dancing and sitting down together. I can expose myself, however, only once more, because he leaves the country soon after next Friday, on which day we are to have a dance at Ashe after all.

Tom Lefroy's feelings for Jane had been serious enough to prompt his uncle and aunt Lefroy, who thought him too young as well as too poor to consider marriage, to send him back home to Ireland. Within a year, Tom was engaged to another woman who was financially more secure.

Tom Lefroy eventually become Lord Chief Justice of Ireland. In his old age, he spoke to a nephew about the affair with Jane Austen. 'He did not state in what her fascination consisted,' said the young man, 'but he said in so many words that he was in love with her, although he qualified his confession by saying it was a boyish love.'

Novel beginnings
And problems with publishers

The first versions of *Sense and Sensibility*, *Pride and Prejudice* and *Northanger Abbey* were written between 1795 and 1798, when Jane Austen was still living at Steventon Rectory (see Happy Home).

During 1795 Jane began a novel in letters called *Elinor and Marianne*, which would become *Sense and Sensibility*, and in October of the following year she started to write *First Impressions*, the original version of *Pride and Prejudice*. Jane's young niece Anna

– who also had pretensions to be a novelist – remembered in later life that, while playing in a nearby room, she would hear Cassandra in fits of laughter as Jane read *First Impressions* aloud to her. Anna (later Anna Lefroy) got to know the story and the people in it, and began to talk of it to others, until the sisters ordered her to keep it a secret. In the course of 1798 Jane wrote a third book called *Susan*, which would eventually become *Northanger Abbey*.

By 1797 *First Impressions* had apparently been read to the Austen family, for on 1 November Jane's father wrote to the London publisher Thomas Cadell to tell him that he was in possession of 'a manuscript novel, comprising 3 vols., about the length of Miss Burney's *Evelina*'. Thomas Cadell was the son of the famous London publisher of the same name who had published works not only by Fanny Burney, but also by a host of other luminaries. These included Edward Gibbon, David Hume, Samuel Johnson and Adam Smith, as well as novelists and poets such as Tobias Smollett, Charlotte Turner Smith and Robert Burns. George Austen asked Cadell whether he would like to see *First Impressions* with a view to publication, perhaps at the author's expense. The response was negative.

In 1803, the manuscript of *Susan* was sold to another London publisher, Benjamin Crosby, for £10 by a Mr Seymour (probably an agent acting for Jane's brother Henry). Intended for immediate publication, the story was advertised by the publisher soon afterwards as '*Susan*, a Novel in 2 Volumes'. However, it never appeared. Crosby seems to have put the novel aside and forgotten about it – or perhaps, for whatever reason, he felt it was the wrong time to publish. Six years later, this lapse led to a brief but acrimonious exchange between the author and publisher.

In April 1809, under the pseudonym of Mrs Ashton Dennis, Jane Austen wrote to Crosby reminding him that in 1803 he had bought a manuscript novel called *Susan* for £10. If it had been lost, she said, the writer could supply another copy. On other hand, if Mr Crosby ignored this letter, she would feel free to try to secure the publication of her work elsewhere.

Crosby wrote to confirm that he still had the manuscript, but said nothing about its publication by him. If any other firm tried to publish it, he would take action against them, he said, but the author could have it back 'for the same as we paid for it'. No satisfactory explanation has been offered for the publisher's inaction, and there was no immediate consequence of his correspondence with the author.

In the event, *Northanger Abbey*, as *Susan* was later renamed, was not published until 1818, after Jane Austen's death, in a joint edition with *Persuasion*.

TALES OF TWO SUSANS

While visiting Bath, the heroine of Jane Austen's novel **Susan** *meets a tall, good-looking young clergyman called Henry Tilney. Tilney is thought to have been based on an amusing and charismatic character called Sydney Smith, whom Jane and Cassandra had met in Bath in 1795 (the year before* **Susan** *was written). Smith, who was also a clergyman, would become one of the most celebrated wits of his day. Another story belonging to this period is* **Lady Susan**, *a short (unpublished) novel by Jane Austen about a fashionable mother's cruel treatment of her daughter. The main character may have been based on Mrs Craven, the maternal grandmother of Mary and Martha Lloyd. She treated her own daughters abysmally, including starving them and locking them up, until they were forced to run away.*

Sydney Smith

Wishful thinking?
Church register reveals Jane Austen's 'marriage'

On 25 August 1936, a letter was published in *The Times* newspaper headed JANE AUSTEN'S 'MARRIAGE'. The correspondent was Henry Henshaw, who identified himself as 'churchwarden' but was also the manager of the Steventon estate, which included the rectory where Jane Austen had lived for the first 25 years of her life.

Henshaw had noticed that in one of the marriage registers in Steventon's church of St Nicholas, which covered the period around 1800, somone had written in the gaps on the specimen page. The name 'Jane Austen' appeared three times on this page of the register: first in a sample 'Publication of Banns', secondly in an 'Entry of Marriage', and third in a sentence confirming the solemnization of a marriage, where it appears in the form 'Jane Smith, late Austen'. The name 'Henry Frederic Howard Fitzwilliam of London' appears beside Jane's in the banns section, while 'Edmund Arthur William Mortimer of Liverpool' appears in a similar position in the marriage section.

It is tempting to believe that, in defacing the specimen page – for the words were undoubtedly in her handwriting – Jane Austen was indulging in some wishful thinking. As it happens, however, there was a straightforward explanation to this apparently puzzling discovery.

In the past, parish registers had been blank books in which baptisms, marriages and burials were recorded haphazardly and often inaccurately. So in the mid-18th century the Church of England introduced a new type of record-keeping using printed books. The pages were laid out with numbered entries and spaces were left to insert individual names and dates. In addition, the Marriage Register had a sample page at the beginning that showed how to fill in the entries for both the calling of the banns and the actual marriage service. It was one of these sample pages, in a volume used by her father, Rev. George Austen, that Jane had been unable to resist filling in.

Although Henshaw questioned whether the names that had been used belonged to anyone Jane in fact knew, he was inclined to believe that it was simply a manifestation of the author's sense of humour. An alternative suggestion is that she carried out the prank to amuse young children, who might be taken in by the entry in the register and believe it to be authentic.

Henry Henshaw explained in his letter why he had chosen to make this revelation in the columns of *The Times*. In 1934, two years earlier, a photograph of Steventon church had been published in the newspaper as part of a restoration appeal. The church's association with Jane Austen had drawn responses from Burma, Peking, Egypt, various parts of the USA, Australia and Ireland. Henshaw therefore felt there was no better place to publish his discovery than in *The Times* newspaper, so that 'Jane-ites' everywhere could learn of it again, as before.

Gold chains and topaz crosses
Gifts from a little brother

On display today in the Admirals' Room at Chawton museum in Hampshire are some prized naval items belonging to Charles Austen (1774–1865), Jane's youngest sibling, whom she once described as 'our own particular little brother'. They include an elaborately carved ceremonial sword given to Charles by the Venezuelan leader Simón Bolívar. The

Topaz cross

inscription on the sword reads: 'Presented to Charles John Austen R.N. commanding HMS *Aurora* at the city of Caracas, 1st March 1827, by General Simón Bolívar the liberator of his country as a mark of esteem.' Also on show is an enormously heavy Burmese bell presented to Charles as commander-in-chief after the storming of Rangoon on 14 April 1852, during the Second Anglo-Burmese War.

Charles, who had entered the Royal Naval Academy in 1791 as a 12-year-old, had risen by the end of his career to the rank of rear-admiral. After serving in the Napoleonic wars, he took part in conflicts in North and South America and the Far East. On 7 October 1852, while still on active service in Burma, he died from cholera aged 73. Early in his career, Charles had been stationed for seven years in the West Indies, where he met and married his first wife, Frances Palmer. He had three children with Frances, who died

HMS Endymion

10£ more – but of what avail is it to take prizes if he lays out the produce in presents to his Sisters. He has been buying Gold chains and Topaze Crosses for us; – he must be well scolded… I shall write again by this post to thank and reproach him. We shall be unbearably fine.

in 1814, and four with his second wife, Harriet Palmer (Frances' sister) whom he married in 1820.

In May 1801, Charles had arrived in Portsmouth aboard HMS *Endymion* with two topaz crosses and gold chains. These were presents for his sisters bought in Gibraltar using his share of prize money from the capture of a French vessel in the Mediterranean. In a similar incident in *Mansfield Park*, Fanny Price is given an amber cross by her brother, William.

Jane Austen adopted a tone of mock reproach when writing to Cassandra about the gifts, which she clearly valued highly:

[Charles] has received 30£ of his share of the privateer & expects

NAVAL CONNECTIONS

Jane Austen's links with the Royal Navy, through her brothers Francis and Charles, influenced her writing. Both **Mansfield Park** *and* **Persuasion** *have strong naval themes, and the character of William Price in* **Mansfield Park**, *Fanny's sailor brother, was probably based on Charles. In* **Persuasion**, *Sir Walter Elliot dislikes the fact that the navy brings 'men of obscure birth into undue distinction', but happily accepts the wealthy Admiral and Mrs Croft as tenants of his family estate, Kellynch Hall. Meanwhile in the same novel Louisa Musgrove is convinced that 'sailors [have] more worth and warmth than any other set of men in England'.*

Strange scandal
Jane Austen's aunt put in prison for theft

In the closing years of the 18th century, when Jane Austen was in her early twenties and still living at Steventon Rectory (see Happy Home), she made regular visits to Bath to see members of her large circle of family and friends. She particularly enjoyed visiting James and Jane Leigh Perrot, her rich and respectable uncle and aunt, who divided their time between Bath and a country house called Scarlets in Berkshire. James was the brother of Jane's mother, Cassandra, who had been born a Leigh; he had altered his name to include that of his future wife, Miss Perrot, an heiress.

In 1799, the Leigh Perrots became embroiled in a strange scandal. On 8 August they went into a haberdasher's shop in Stall Street, Bath, where Mrs Leigh Perrot bought a length of black lace. On leaving the shop she was followed and stopped by the shopkeeper, who accused her of taking some white lace that she had not paid for. Opening the packet, she discovered that the white lace was there, alongside the black, and handed it back, saying that there must have been a mistake.

A few days later, Mrs Leigh Perrot was arrested for theft. The shopkeeper had laid a charge against her of stealing lace to the value of 20 shillings. She was taken off to the local gaol at Ilchester to await trial at the next assizes. Needless to say, a prison in those days was a very unpleasant and dangerous place, and far removed from anything that a gentlewoman such as Mrs Leigh Perrot would ever have experienced.

Mr Leigh Perrot, who insisted on staying with his wife, persuaded the gaoler to put them up in his own house until the time of the trial. Though better than the prison, the lodgings were cramped, dirty and noisy. Since bail was refused, the couple had to endure the squalid conditions for seven months. Stealing anything over the value of 5 shillings was a capital offence, so the Leigh Perrots knew that, if

Jane Leigh Perrot

creatures gazed at in a public court would cut one to the very heart'.

When the trial finally took place at Taunton on 29 March 1800, the jury found Mrs Leigh Perrot not guilty and she was released. The most likely explanation for this strange episode is that the shopkeeper, an unreliable character who was in financial difficulties, had contrived to bring the charge in the belief that Mr Leigh Perrot would be ready to pay him a large sum to withdraw it. In the event, Jane's uncle made it clear that he would never submit to blackmail of this kind, and the attempt to extort money as a bribe to avoid prosecution fell flat on its face.

convicted, Mrs Leigh Perrot would probably be sent to the penal colony in Botany Bay, Australia, for up to 14 years.

Mrs Austen suggested that, during this traumatic period, Jane and Cassandra might stay with their aunt in prison to provide her with companionship and, later, support her at her trial. But Mrs Leigh Perrot refused both offers, saying of the second: 'to have two young

'It's all settled!'
Shocking news of the move to Bath

Jane Austen's early literary period ended with a dramatic change in her family's living arrangements. On 30 November 1800, after spending a few days with the Lloyds at Ibthorpe (see Good Friends), Jane returned home to Steventon, bringing Martha Lloyd with her. As they entered the house, Mrs Austen greeted them with the words 'Well, girls! It's all settled. We have decided to leave Steventon and go to Bath.'

The Rev. George Austen was nearing 70 and had probably been considering retirement for some time, especially since his son James was ready to take over the Steventon living. Yet Jane had received no warning of the momentous decision. On hearing the news she collapsed in a faint, overcome by shock.

Jane Austen's reaction reveals the strength of her feelings about leaving the only home she had ever known, as well as misgivings about the destination her parents had chosen. Although two of her novels were largely set in Bath, Jane had little affection for the place. When she and her sister, Cassandra, had first visited in the early 1790s, Bath was no longer the fashionable resort it had been 50 years earlier.

Instead it had become a solid, respectable town, visited by those who were keen to improve their health rather than by pleasure-seekers. Yet it was still popular with the country gentry, who flocked in the evening to theatrical performances or balls and concerts at the Assembly Rooms, and spent their days window-shopping, meeting friends in the Pump Room or visiting local beauty spots.

Although Jane Austen enjoyed social activities of this kind, she would never be really at home in the city. Indeed, the novelist seems to have felt rather like her own character Anne Elliott in *Persuasion*, who had 'a very determined, though silent, disinclination for Bath'. The city might have been an exciting introduction to the adult world for an unsophisticated girl such as Catherine Morland of *Northanger Abbey*, but it had little to offer those of a more mature and adventurous nature.

So, in May 1801, Mr and Mrs Austen and their two daughters, Jane and Cassandra, moved to Bath, at first staying in the Paragon with Mrs Austen's relations the Leigh Perrots and eventually settling at 4 Sydney Place, overlooking the fashionable Sydney Gardens. The years at Bath were comparatively

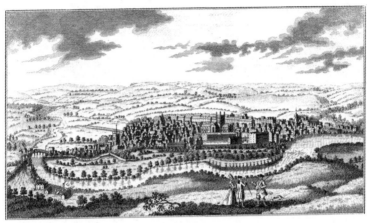

Bath in 1784

uneventful, enlivened only by family visits and tours to the seaside – to Dawlish, Teignmouth and Ramsgate – as well as some romantic encounters.

In 1804 the family left Sydney Place for a house in Green Park Buildings, nearer to the Pump Room. This was for the benefit of George Austen, who could by that time walk only with a stick. After George's death in 1805, the women took up residence in 25 Gay Street, a smaller house needing only one maid. They were joined there by Martha Lloyd, whose mother had died at Ibthorp in April the same year.

The Austens made one more move in Bath. In April 1806 they were in Trim Street and then, in June, they went to Clifton, a village near Bristol, leaving Bath for ever. In 1808, Jane wrote to Cassandra, 'It will be two years tomorrow since we left Bath for Clifton, with what happy feelings of escape!'

Affaires of the heart
Jane Austen has a sudden change of mind

In November 1802, Jane and Cassandra Austen had been staying with their close friends the Bigg-Withers at Manydown in Hampshire, not far from Steventon. Early on 3 December the sisters appeared at Steventon Rectory in an agitated state, insisting that their brother James should drive them back home to Bath the next day. To meet this request, James Austen, who had succeeded his father as rector a year earlier, had to find a substitute to preach for him that Sunday.

During the journey back home to Bath, it emerged that Harris Bigg-Wither had proposed to Jane the night before and had been accepted. Despite the discrepancy in age – he was 21 and she was 27 – it would seem to have been a good match. But in the morning Jane realized that she could not go through with it. Her niece Caroline said long afterwards, 'To be sure she should not have said

"Yes" overnight, but I have always respected her for cancelling that "Yes" the next morning.'

The sequence of events leading up to this drama may have had its roots in the summer of 1801, when the Austen sisters and their parents took a seaside holiday at Sidmouth in Devon. There, Jane met a young man who was strongly attracted to her, and the attraction was reciprocated. Almost nothing is known about this man, but Cassandra found him handsome, intelligent and charming – and, above all, good enough for her sister. After the pair had known each other for less than three weeks, the man had to leave Sidmouth urgently. The next news they had was a letter from his brother saying that he had suddenly died – and that was it.

Jane's emotions can only be guessed at, since no letters written by her immediately following this event have survived, but some people believe that the impact of her brief romance at Sidmouth may have proved a great deal stronger than she might have foreseen.

Lure of Lyme
The Cobb inspires a scene of high drama

Harris Bigg-Wither

Lyme Regis in Dorset was the site of a memorable holiday that Jane Austen took with her parents in 1804. Jane's letters to her sister Cassandra, who was in Weymouth at the time, include references to walks along the Cobb – the harbour wall – where years later she would imagine Louisa Musgrove's dramatic accident in *Persuasion* (chapter 12).

This meant that, when Harris Bigg-Wither made his proposal of marriage, the memory of her former love was still so vivid that she could not help comparing her two suitors. Although Harris had many good qualities, including wealth and social status, Jane felt unable to dedicate her life to him while she was still in love with someone else.

Equally, Jane's rejection of Harris may have sprung from a conscious or unconscious realization that, in accepting the yoke of a traditional marriage, she would never be able to fulfil her destiny as a writer.

The beauty of Lyme made a deep impression on the novelist. She particularly loved the scenery around Charmouth with 'its sweet retired bay backed by dark cliffs, where fragments of low rock among the sands make it the happiest spot for watching the flow of the tide, for sitting in unwearied contemplation'.

Visiting Lyme in 1867, the poet laureate Alfred Lord Tennyson is said to have gone straight to the Cobb on his arrival, saying, 'Show me the exact spot where Louisa Musgrove fell!' This is how Jane described the incident in

North view of Lyme Cobb in 1823

Persuasion. Thankfully, contrary to the impression given in this extract, Louisa survived the fall:

> There was too much wind to make the high part of the new Cobb pleasant for the ladies, and they agreed to get down the steps to the lower, and all were contented to pass quietly and carefully down the steep flight, excepting Louisa; she must be jumped down them by Captain Wentworth. In all their walks, he had had to jump her from the stiles; the sensation was delightful to her. The hardness of the pavement for her feet, made him less willing upon the present occasion; he did it, however. She was safely down, and instantly, to show her enjoyment, ran up the steps to be jumped down again. He advised her against it, thought the jar too great; but no, he reasoned and talked in vain, she smiled and said, "I am determined I will:" he put out his hands; she was too precipitate by half a second, she fell on the pavement on the Lower Cobb, and was taken up lifeless!

THE WATSONS ORIGINAL SOLD FOR £850,000

During the five years she lived in Bath, Jane Austen started work on only one original novel, which she abandoned in 1805 after writing only 17,500 words. This novel, in its unfinished form, would make its appearance long after her death as **The Watsons***. Nine authors have since written completions of the novel with varying degrees of success. The first of these was Jane's niece Catherine Hubback, daughter of Frank Austen, whose version was published in the mid-19th century under the title* **The Younger Sister***. In 2011 Sotheby's auctioneers sold Austen's original manuscript of* **The Watsons** *to the Bodleian Library in Oxford for £850,000.*

Sudden death
Close confidante falls from her horse

On 16 December 1804, on Jane Austen's 29th birthday, her great friend Anne Lefroy, the widow of the Rev. Isaac Lefroy of Ashe near Steventon, was killed in a fall from a horse at the age of 55. Known as Madam Lefroy for her sophisticated tastes and manners, Anne had become a close confidante of Jane, despite the 26-year difference in their ages.

As a great reader (and writer) of poetry, Anne Lefroy had allowed Jane access to the extensive library at Ashe Rectory. She used her relative wealth for philanthropic purposes, doing welfare work among the poor children of the neighbourhood and teaching them to read and write. A pioneer in health matters, she even vaccinated 800 children with her own hands.

Tom Lefroy, a nephew of the Lefroys of Ashe, was one of Jane Austen's first loves (see The Tom Lefroy Affair). However his aunt and uncle had discouraged the young couple's relationship, fearing that it was doomed to failure because neither of them had enough money.

In the opinion of Jane's nephew Edward Austen-Leigh and others, Madam Lefroy was a remarkable person. 'Her rare endowments of goodness, talents, graceful person, and engaging manners, were sufficient to secure her a prominent place in any society into which she was thrown,' wrote Edward, 'while her enthusiastic eagerness of disposition rendered her especially attractive to a clever and lively girl.'

Jane Austen's sadness at the death of her old friend prompted her to write her only known serious poem. Although it has little literary merit, the poem reveals what a deep impression Madam Lefroy had made on the budding author – and what a bitter blow her loss must have been – as this extract shows:

I see her here with all her
   smiles benign,
Her looks of eager love, her
   accents sweet.
That voice and countenance
   almost divine,

Expression, harmony, alike
   complete…

Hers is the energy of soul
   sincere;
Her Christian spirit, ignorant
   to feign,
Seek but to comfort, heal,
   enlighten, cheer,
Confer a pleasure or prevent
   a pain.

To the rescue
*Austen brothers avert
a financial crisis*

The Rev. George Austen died on 21 January 1805, aged 74, after a fleeting illness. 'We have lost an excellent father,' wrote Jane in a letter to her brother Frank. 'His tenderness…who can do justice to [it]?' Before the burial at the Church of St Swithin at Walcot, Bath, where he had married Cassandra Leigh four decades earlier, George's coffin was left open for mourners to view the body. 'The serenity of the corpse is most delightful!' wrote Jane. 'It preserves the sweet, benevolent smile which

Church of St Swithin at Walcot, Bath

always distinguished him.'

Until George Austen's death, his family had been comfortably off, able to maintain a household with a manservant and two maids, but the greater part of his income died with him. Mrs Austen and her daughters now had just £210 a year, including the interest on the £1,000 left to Cassandra by her late suitor, Thomas Fowle (see Death in the Caribbean).

In the event, the sudden financial crisis revealed the members of the Austen family at their most generous and most solicitous about the welfare of others. James and Henry each volunteered to give their mother £50 a year, to which Edward (the wealthiest) added £100. Frank offered another £100 but, when his mother found out, she refused to take more than £50 from him. (Charles was away in the West Indies.) Owing to her sons' generosity, Mrs Austen now had an income amounting to £460 a year. 'Never were children so good as mine!' she insisted.

FRANK MISSES BATTLE OF TRAFALGAR

In 1805, Jane's brother Frank, a naval captain, narrowly missed taking part in the Battle of Trafalgar because, at the crucial moment, he had been ordered to go

Horatio Nelson

to Gibraltar to oversee the conveyance of military supplies. Earlier described by Nelson as 'an excellent young man', Frank was devastated by his bad luck, writing to his fiancée, 'To lose all share in the glory of a day which surpasses all which ever went before is what I cannot think of with any degree of patience.' Little did Frank know that he was on the brink of a stellar naval career, which would eventually see him rise to the topmost ranks of the Royal Navy (see Seaside Interlude).

Opulent magnificence
Austen women visit Adlestrop and Stoneleigh

After leaving Bath in early 1806, Mrs Austen and her daughters lodged briefly in Clifton, near Bristol, while contemplating a move to Southampton, where they planned to live temporarily with Frank Austen and his new wife, Mary. Before taking up residence in Southampton, however, they accepted an invitation to visit Mrs

Adlestrop House in Gloucestershire

Austen's cousin, the Rev. Thomas Leigh, at his Adlestrop estate in Gloucestershire, where the landscape designer Humphry Repton had recently carried out improvements. In the event, their stay at Adlestrop was all too short.

Following the death of a distant relation who had been a sister of the last Lord Leigh, Thomas Leigh set off for Stoneleigh Abbey in Warwickshire to claim his rightful inheritance. Since Lord Leigh had left a will that was capable of misinterpretation, Thomas had been advised to take possession of Stoneleigh immediately – and the Austen women accompanied him on the mission. For Cassandra and Jane, it was a rare opportunity to experience aristocratic life on a magnificent scale.

In a letter to an Austen family friend, Mary Lloyd, Mrs Austen described the experience of 'Eating fish, venison & all manner of good things in a noble large parlour hung round with family pictures.' She was amazed by the beauty of the grounds and the vastness of the house, which had '26 bed chambers in the new part…and a great many in the old'.

Other members of the Leigh family were included in the house party, including a foolish and talkative character called Lady Saye and Sele, whose headdress had once been described by the novelist Fanny Burney as 'full of feathers and flowers and jewels and jee-gaws'. She was a great source of entertainment to some of the other guests. 'Poor Lady Saye and Sele to be sure is rather tormenting,' wrote Mrs Austen, 'though sometimes amusing and affords Jane many a good laugh: but she fatigues me sadly.'

MOCK-GOTHIC PHANTASM

Soon after their arrival in Southampton in the autumn of 1806, Mrs Austen and her daughters, along with her son Frank and his wife Mary, moved into a large house with its own garden in Castle Square, rented from the Marquess of Lansdowne. In the middle of the square was a miniature mock-gothic castle that Lord Lansdowne had built for his wife. The Austens were highly amused each morning to see from their windows the extraordinary sight of the marchioness driving out from the miniature castle in a light phaeton drawn by eight long-tailed ponies in various shades of brown, with two boys in smart livery riding postillion.

Seaside interlude
*Frank Austen's prestigious
79-year naval career*

Jane's brother Francis Austen, known to the family as Frank, had joined the Royal Navy in 1786, at the age of 12, and risen rapidly through the ranks. On the outbreak of the war with Napoleon in 1803, he took responsibility for organizing a naval defence force at Ramsgate on the Kent coast. He later became commanding officer of HMS *Canopus*, in which he fought at the Battle of Santo Domingo in the Caribbean. Frank observed the Battle of Vimeiro from his ship HMS *St Albans* before taking aboard British troops who were retreating after the Battle of Corunna. He would go on to be commanding officer of HMS *Elephant* and to capture the American privateer *Swordfish* during the War of 1812.

Since Mrs Austen and his sisters had nowhere permanent to live after the death of his father in 1805, Frank suggested that they share a

Southampton in the 19th century

home with him in Southampton, which was, for him, conveniently close to the fleet at Portsmouth. At the time of their arrival, Frank had recently married his long-term sweetheart, Mary Gibson.

From the house they rented in Castle Square, the Austen family enjoyed regular walks on the promenade along the old city walls of Southampton. They made excursions by boat on the River Itchen to see warships being built at Northam and the Gothic ruins of Netley Abbey. They also took boat trips to the New Forest and up the Beaulieu river past Buckler's Hard and Beaulieu Abbey.

These waterside outings have a flavour of the scenes at Portsmouth in *Mansfield Park* and at Lyme Regis in *Persuasion*. In *Mansfield Park* the only thing Fanny Price appreciated in Portsmouth was, on a bright March day, 'the effects of the shadows pursuing each other on the ships at Spithead and the island beyond, with the ever varying hues of the sea, now at high water, dancing in its glee and dashing against the ramparts'.

Jane Austen took long walks through the countryside around Southampton, beside Southampton Water and along the banks of the Itchen and Test rivers. She and Cassandra amused themselves in the evening by attending dances, including some in the upstairs room of the Dolphin Hotel. They enjoyed spending several months with Frank and his family, and gaining an insight into naval life. Apart from the fact that he was excellent company, Frank was an enthusiastic and skilled handyman – this aspect of his character, Jane said, influenced her portrayal of Captain Harville in *Persuasion*.

The pleasant interlude could not last for ever. Frank was obliged to return to sea, and by the autumn of 1808 Mrs Austen and her daughters had decided to leave Southampton and find their own home, where they would live for many years with their good friend Martha Lloyd. As it transpired, two decades later Martha Lloyd became Frank Austen's second wife, following the death of Mary, with whom he had seven children.

In 1837 Frank was knighted, and a few years later he was appointed commander-in-chief of the North America and West Indies Station. There his main role was to protect British commercial interests during the Mexican–American War of 1846–47 and to disrupt the activities of slave traders. Made a full admiral on 1 August 1848, Frank was promoted to Admiral of the Fleet on 27 April 1863. He died in the post two years later, at the age of 91, ending a naval career that had spanned 79 years.

A GIRL 'AFTER ONE'S OWN HEART'

In 1808 Jane and Cassandra Austen stayed on separate occasions with their brother Edward and his family at Godmersham in Kent. Since his marriage in 1791 to Elizabeth Bridges, Edward had fathered many children, the eldest of whom was a daughter, Fanny. During her visit in spring 1808, Jane struck up an intense friendship with 15-year-old Fanny. 'I could not have supposed that a niece would ever have been so much to me,' she wrote to Cassandra, 'She is quite after one's own heart.' Cassandra's visit later in the year ended in tragedy, however. On 28 September a son, Brook John, was born to Edward and Elizabeth. At first Elizabeth seemed to be doing well, but she suddenly became seriously ill, and on 10 October she died, depriving 11 children of a devoted mother.

Centre of creativity
The final move to Chawton

When the widowed Mrs Austen decided to leave Southampton and set up home elsewhere with her two daughters (see Seaside Interlude), her son Edward, who had inherited money and estates from his adoptive father, Thomas Knight (see Chosen as Heir), entered the fray. Edward wanted to find his mother and sisters a home on his own property where he could ensure that they were well looked after. He offered them a choice of two houses, one

Chawton cottage today

in Kent near Godmersham, and the other in Hampshire at Chawton, a mile from Alton. The second option was eventually decided upon; it was familiar territory and only a morning's ride from the family's old haunts at Steventon.

Writing in 1870, Edward Austen-Leigh described his impression of the cottage at Chawton to which his grandmother and two aunts moved in 1809, with their friend Martha Lloyd. 'It was so close to the road that the front door opened upon it,' he wrote, 'while a very narrow enclosure, paled in on each side, protected the

building from danger of collision with any runaway vehicle.' Austen-Leigh explained that the house had once been an inn, but recent improvements by its owner, Jane's brother Edward, had made it 'a pleasant and commodious abode'.

In recognition of his inheritance from the Knight family, Jane's brother Edward had adopted the surname Knight. In the words of Edward Austen-Leigh:

Mr Knight was experienced and adroit at such arrangements, and this was a labour of love to him. A good-sized entrance and two sitting-rooms made the length of the house, all intended originally to look upon the road, but the large drawing-room window was blocked up and turned into a book-case, and another opened at the side which gave to view only turf and trees, as a high wooden fence and hornbeam hedge shut out the Winchester road, which skirted the whole length of the little domain. Trees were planted each side to form a shrubbery walk, carried round the enclosure, which gave a sufficient space for ladies' exercise. There was a pleasant irregular mixture of hedgerow, and gravel walk, and orchard, and long grass for mowing, arising from two or three little enclosures having been thrown together.

Chawton was the place where Jane Austen revised the text of her first three novels and wrote three new ones, *Mansfield Park*, *Emma* and *Persuasion*. The house is now a museum dedicated to the author's memory.

Solitary sketch
Few images of the author remain

Tantalizingly, only one indisputably authentic portrait of Jane Austen has survived – an unfinished sketch by her sister, Cassandra. Many viewers believe that this is not a good likeness, since the features seem to be too sharp and crude to represent the Austen revealed to us through her writing.

When Edward Austen-Leigh decided to have Cassandra's sketch engraved for inclusion in the

Engraving of Jane Austen, based on Cassandra's sketch

memoir he wrote of his aunt Jane, published in 1870, his siblings and cousins made known their disapproval, clearly believing that the resulting portrait did not do justice to the author. Even though the engraving makes Jane's features softer and gentler than in the original sketch, Austen-Leigh was forced to admit that 'perhaps it gave some idea of the truth [rather than the whole truth]'.

In fact, it is Edward Austen-Leigh's own words that bring his aunt more to life than any other description:

> In person she was very attractive; her figures was rather tall and slender, her step light and firm, and her whole appearance expressive of health and animation. In complexion she was a clear brunette with a rich colour; she had full round cheeks, with mouth and nose well formed, bright hazel eyes, and brown hair forming natural curls round her face. If not so regularly handsome as her sister, yet her countenance had a peculiar

charm of its own to the eyes of most beholders.

Jane Austen's attractiveness is well captured visually in a silhouette found in 1944 pasted into a volume of the second edition of *Mansfield Park*, with *'L'aimable Jane'* written in an unknown hand. The Austen scholar R. W. Chapman was convinced that this image showed the author – but Chapman rejected claims that the full-length 'Rice portrait', supposedly painted in 1788 by Ozias Humphry, was a representation of Jane Austen at the age of 13. The Rice family had inherited this picture from descendants of Jane's great uncle, Francis Austen, but in 1948 its authenticity was disputed on costume grounds. Some said that the high waist and sash shown in the portrait did not become popular in England until around 1805, when Jane Austen was 30, and the controversy continues.

In 2011 another Austen scholar, Paula Byrne, claimed to have discovered a lost portrait that showed the novelist as a professional woman writer, proud and confident. The portrait was the subject of a BBC documentary, in which two out of three experts argued that it was authentic, but this cannot be established beyond doubt.

SAVED BY A CREAKY DOOR

Jane Austen went to great lengths to conceal the fact that she was a writer, even from friends and servants. Her neighbours at Chawton cottage knew her only as the daughter of a former rector of Steventon, and at home nobody was aware of her literary work except her closest relations and her family's good friend Martha Lloyd. She had no private room to write in, choosing to work in the dining room at a little table on which she had placed her mahogany writing slope. She wrote on small pieces of paper because this made it easier for her, if interrupted, to slip them into a drawer or under the blotter. Her only protection was a door that creaked loudly when opened – which she refused to have repaired

since it alerted her that someone was coming and gave her time to hide her writing materials.

First publication
Jane Austen 'never too busy to think of S & S'

*S*ense and Sensibility: A novel in three volumes by a Lady was Jane Austen's first book to appear in print. It was well received enough to make a small profit – much to the author's surprise. The manuscript, a revision of the earlier *Elinor and Marianne*, had been sold in 1810 to Thomas Egerton of the Military Library. There was a family link with this publisher, in that Egerton had previously printed *The Loiterer*, the periodical edited by James and Henry Austen during their time at Oxford (see *The Loiterer*).

Jane Austen had been asked to pay for publication of *Sense and Sensibility* on a commission basis, as was common at the time. Egerton would put up the initial money, then Jane would be paid only after the printing costs and publisher's

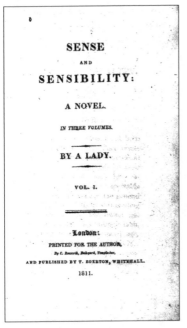

Title page from the first edition of Sense and Sensibility

February 1811, she had started writing *Mansfield Park*, but it was *Sense and Sensibility* that was still uppermost in her mind. She began working on the proofs in April, while staying at 64 Sloane Street in Knightsbridge with her brother Henry and his wife, Eliza.

When Cassandra asked in a letter whether her sister was too busy to think about her forthcoming book, Jane replied, 'No indeed, I am never too busy to think of S & S. I can no more forget it, than a mother can forget her sucking child.' She went on to express her irritation that the editing process took so long: 'I have had two sheets to correct, but the last only brings us to W.s. [Willoughby's] first appearance... I have scarcely a hope of its being out in June.' Jane was right to have her doubts about the publication date. In the event, the book appeared five months later than originally scheduled, in November 1811.

commission had been recouped. It was understood that the author would reimburse the publisher for any loss – which, in this case, proved unnecessary.

Jane was heavily involved in editing and preparing the text for publication. It is probable that, by

BEGINNER'S MODESTY

The first published account of Jane Austen's life was written by her brother Henry and appeared in 1818, as a preface to a joint edition of Northanger Abbey *and* Persuasion *that was published posthumously. 'An invincible distrust of her own judgement induced her to withhold her works from the public,' wrote Henry. Jane had taken up writing 'entirely from taste and inclination', but she was so doubtful about the merit of her first novel,* Sense and Sensibility, *that she could hardly believe her 'great good fortune' when the book made a profit of £150. The author's identity was kept secret, even from her family. Jane's niece Anna, who noticed a copy of the novel in a circulating library, declared – in the presence of her aunt – that, with such a title, the book must be rubbish.*

'My own darling child'
Pride and Prejudice *is printed*

Jane Austen's ecstasy on receiving her first printed copy of *Pride and Prejudice* is all too evident in her correspondence with her sister, Cassandra. In a letter dated 29 January 1813, she described the book as 'my own darling child' just arrived from London. 'On Wednesday I received one copy sent down by Falkener [the proprietor of the London to Southampton coach service],' she wrote, 'with three lines from Henry to say that he had given another to Charles and sent a third by the coach to Godmersham.'

Having examined the volume carefully – and no doubt read every word of it – she was moved to comment on its length, explaining that a lot of editing had been required: 'I have lop't and crop't so successfully that I imagine it must be rather shorter than *Sense and Sensibility*.' Her greatest thrill was the successful portrayal of the character Elizabeth Bennet: 'I must confess that I think her as delightful a creature as ever appeared in print,

Elizabeth Bennet and Mr Wickham in Pride and Prejudice

on writing, a critique on Walter Scott, of the history of Buonaparté, or something that would form a contrast.' The point of such a contrast, said the author, would be to 'bring the reader with increased delight to the playfulness and epigrammatism of the general style'.

Later in February, she wrote again to Cassandra to thank her sister for describing the delight and amusement that *Pride and Prejudice* had given her. 'I am exceedingly pleased that you can say what you do, after having gone through the whole work,' she said, remarking that she was equally pleased to hear how much her niece Fanny had liked the book: 'Fanny's praise is very gratifying. My hopes were tolerably strong of *her*, but nothing like a certainty. Her liking Darcy and Elizabeth is enough. She might hate all the others if she would.'

and how I shall be able to tolerate those who do not like her at least I do not know.'

A week later she sent another letter to Cassandra with a more detailed critique of her own novel, including a complaint about printer's errors. 'The work is rather too light, and bright, and sparkling; it wants shade,' she wrote. 'It wants to be stretched out here and there with a long chapter of sense, if it could be had; if not, of solemn specious nonsense, about something unconnected with the story; an essay

Authorship revealed
*Brotherly vanity gets the
better of Henry*

Following the publication of
Pride and Prejudice in January
1813, Jane Austen was anxious
to keep her identity as author
hidden. Yet the book's enthusiastic
reception by the critics and
the reading public meant that
speculation was rife. Rumours
began to circulate in Chawton, but
it was Jane's brother Henry who
revealed the secret while staying
with friends in Scotland. Jane
explained what had happened in a
letter to her brother Frank:

Henry heard P. & P. warmly
praised in Scotland, by Lady
Robert Kerr and another lady;
and what does he do in the
warmth of his brotherly vanity
and love, but immediately tell
them who wrote it! A thing
once set going in that way – one
knows how it spreads! – and he,
dear creature, has set it going so
much more than once.

Henry was Jane's favourite brother,
so she was prepared to forgive him
most things, believing, as she told
Frank, that he acted always out of
'affection & partiality'. Brimming
with wit and charisma, Henry was
a substantial influence on Jane's life.
His niece Anna Lefroy wrote of him:

He was the handsomest of the
family, and in the opinion of
his father, the most talented.
There were others who formed
a different opinion, but, for
the most part, he was greatly
admired. Brilliant in conversation
he was, and, like his father,
blessed with a hopefulness of
temper which, in adapting itself
to all circumstances, served to
create a perpetual sunshine.

This optimism led Henry always
to think that his next move was
bound to be successful, but it was
combined with an apparent inability
to stick to any chosen course of
action. During his youth, Henry
had appeared the most promising
of all the Austens, not least on
the intellectual front, and, like his

elder brother James, he went up to Oxford in 1788. Henry also had an infectious gaiety that made him the life and soul of the party. He had several careers that included serving in the Oxfordshire Militia, co-founding the bank Austen, Maunde & Tilson, and becoming a clergyman. Although he tired of soldiering, failed as a banker, and made no great name for himself in the church, he somehow always managed to recover from failure and disappointment.

Perhaps Henry Austen's greatest gift to posterity was to act as Jane Austen's unofficial literary agent and to oversee the publication of her novels. In 1818 he wrote the first 'biographical notice' of his sister, which was included in the posthumously published joint edition of *Northanger Abbey* and *Persuasion*.

Henry Austen married his widowed cousin Eliza de Feuillide in 1797 and Eleanor Jackson in 1820, but he had no children.

Comic spirit
Jane Austen, empathy and learning the art of living well

Critics of Jane Austen point out that, even though she lived through the period of the French Revolution and the Napoleonic Wars, no direct reference to these cataclysmic events or similar crises appears in her books. She could hardly fail to be aware of them, especially since they touched her own family; her cousin by marriage had been guillotined (see 'Enemy of the Republic' Guillotined) and two of her brothers were fighting in the wars (see Gold Chains and Topaz Crosses and Seaside Interlude). It seems, however, that – either instinctively or by design – Jane Austen excluded any subject matter incompatible with the comic spirit that she used to create empathy in her readers.

In *Letters to Alice on first reading Jane Austen*, published in 1984, Fay Weldon addresses this question in a fictional correspondence between an aunt and her niece. Pointing out that the first version of *Pride and*

Prejudice was written in 1796, a year of famine, shortages and mass rural unemployment, the aunt queries why intelligent readers should be expected to take seriously a narrative that – while ignoring these major upheavals – presents us instead with a double love story and a few light-hearted subplots, and ends with everyone apparently living happily ever afterwards.

Fay Weldon's 'aunt', who is also the book's narrator, responds to her own query by defining why reading fiction is important, whoever you are. She explains that it widens our horizons, deepens our understanding of humanity, and makes us more aware of what motivates ourselves and the people around us.

The narrator goes on to argue that Jane Austen is one of the supreme exponents of fiction in the English language – and that *Pride and Prejudice* and Austen's other novels allow her readers to learn and appreciate time and again how to empathize with other people. Much of this effect is achieved, of course, through the medium

of satire and comedy, as well as by gentle moral instruction. It is only by practising empathy on a daily basis, insists the narrator, that human beings can become better at the art of living.

NEPHEW ASTONISHED

Jane Austen loved to spend time with her nephews and nieces, particularly Edward Austen-Leigh (born in 1798), who lived at Steventon Rectory after his father, James, had taken on the Steventon living. Aunt and nephew had been brought together by her novels, of which Edward had much enjoyed the first two. As a child he had not been told of their authorship. However, some time in 1814, Edward sent his aunt a poem revealing his astonishment on discovering the truth. Here is an extract:

> *Oh dear, just to think (and the thought drives me mad)*
> *That dear Mrs Jennings' good-natured strain*
> *Was really the produce of your*

witty brain,
That you made the Middletons,
Dashwoods and all…
And though Mr Collins so
grateful for all
Will Lady de Bourgh his dear
patroness call,
'Tis to your ingenuity really
he owed
His living, his wife, and his
humble abode.

Universal truths
Evoking a world in the
first sentence

Jane Austen was the mistress of many literary arts. But the one most studied and imitated by aspiring novelists is the art of the first sentence – which she used, apparently effortlessly, to evoke a whole world.

The opening two sentences of *Sense and Sensibility* plunge the reader into a distinctive social milieu: 'The family of Dashwood had long been settled in Sussex. Their estate was large, and their residence was at Norland Park, in the centre of their property, where, for many generations, they had lived in so respectable a manner as to engage the general good opinion of their surrounding acquaintance.' The gentle irony in the phrases 'so respectable a manner' and 'general good opinion' signal that the settled calm evoked in this description is not to be relied upon and will soon be disturbed.

Tantalizingly, Austen's most famous opening sentence, at the start of *Pride and Prejudice*, does not mention an individual or a family by name: 'It is a truth universally acknowledged, that a single man in possession of a good fortune, must be in want of a wife.' Although the emphasis here is on universality, it is immediately clear that the novel will examine the validity of this 'truth' through the prism of particular individuals and their families.

The opening of *Mansfield Park* is more direct, describing a precise situation involving an individual who has risen up the social ranks: 'About thirty years ago, Miss Maria Ward of Huntingdon, with only seven thousand pounds, had the good luck to captivate Sir Thomas Bertram, of Mansfield Park, in the county of Northamptonshire, and to be thereby raised to the rank of a baronet's lady, with all the comforts and consequences of an handsome house and large income.' The reader is left in no doubt that this is a book about money, class and social dislocation – with all the intimations of universality attendant on those subjects.

Emma, by contrast, focuses on a single powerful individual who will dominate the action from beginning to end: 'Emma Woodhouse, handsome, clever, and rich, with a comfortable home and happy disposition, seemed to unite some of the best blessings of existence; and had lived nearly twenty-one years in the world with very little to distress or vex her.' Emma's character as delineated is too good to be true, of course, and we know that during the course of the novel it will have to be torn apart and reconstructed into a mature and satisfactory whole – a common human experience.

In *Northanger Abbey*, the leading character is introduced in the first sentence, but in anti-heroic terms: 'No one who had ever seen Catherine Morland in her infancy would have supposed her born to be an heroine.' Why not? Well, nothing is what is seems. We are apparently entering the world of the Gothic novel, but it is presented ironically and all its superficial features are, in the end, found to be misleading.

Finally, the opening sentence of *Persuasion*, much longer than those of the other novels, gives us a vivid picture of the vain, pretentious Sir Walter, who is set up to act as a foil to the much more sympathetic characters, Anne Elliot and Captain Wentworth:

> Sir Walter Elliot, of Kellynch Hall, in Somersetshire, was a man who, for his own amusement, never took up any book but the Baronetage; there he found occupation for an idle hour, and consolation in a distressed one; there his faculties were roused into admiration and respect,

by contemplating the limited remnant of the earliest patents; there any unwelcome sensations, arising from domestic affairs changed naturally into pity and contempt as he turned over the almost endless creations of the last century; and there, if every other leaf were powerless, he could read his own history with an interest which never failed.

It is the unravelling of illusions – both Sir Walter's illusions and those of other characters – that lies at the heart of *Persuasion*.

Mixed reactions
Mansfield Park *pioneers the theme of meritocracy*

In March 1814 Jane Austen was driving to London with her brother Henry. When they reached the village of Bentley Green to the west of Farnham in Surrey, she began to read *Mansfield Park* aloud to him and continued until they reached the point where Maria Bertram marries James Rushworth. Henry was so captivated that he continued reading the manuscript when he got home. 'He admires H. Crawford: I mean properly, as a clever, pleasant man,' wrote Jane to Cassandra.

Mansfield Park: A novel in three volumes by the author of 'Sense and Sensibility' and 'Pride and Prejudice' was published by Thomas Egerton in May 1814 and the first edition of 1,500 copies was sold out within six months. Jane Austen recorded the opinions of family and friends, so it is known that Anna Austen (later Lefroy) did not like the character of Fanny Price, that Fanny Knight wanted 'more love between [Fanny Price] and Edmund', and that Egerton the publisher praised the book for 'its morality, and for being so equal a composition – no weak parts'.

In the intervening years, *Mansfield Park* has continued to elicit mixed reactions, principally because, unlike Jane Austen's other works, it is based on the theme of meritocracy and raises serious questions about wealth, class and social justice.

For a start, the building known

as *Mansfield Park* is different from the great old country houses that feature in other Austen novels, such as Pemberley in *Pride and Prejudice* and Donwell Abbey in *Emma*, in that it is newly built – and its construction was financed from the proceeds of the slave trade. The house belongs to Sir Thomas Bertram, who is introduced to the reader as a benefactor, but – in a manifestation of the powerful moral undercurrents running throughout the narrative – is revealed to own plantations in Antigua.

Henry Crawford and Fanny Price in Mansfield Park

Fanny Price, a poor niece of Sir Thomas, is only ten when she is uprooted from her modest home in Portsmouth, and finds herself in a mansion where she is bullied and ignored. Fanny's anti-heroic qualities make her an excellent foil for the glamorous and dynamic visitors from London, Henry and Mary Crawford, who cause chaos by organizing private theatricals that create opportunities for flirtation. All sorts of tangled relationships ensue, but in the end it is Fanny's steadfastness and strength of character that win through and allow her to overcome the disadvantages of her early life.

Jane Austen strongly believed in the claims of merit and talent over social position and inherited wealth, and this novel is a supreme exposition of that belief. At the start, Sir Thomas is keen that Fanny should know her place – she is not to be treated as 'a Miss Bertram'. But by the end he has come to appreciate 'the advantages of early hardship and discipline, and the consciousness of being born to struggle and endure'.

Delightful pilgrimage
*Cottesbrooke Hall and
Mansfield Park*

Mansfield Park in the eponymous novel is believed to be based on Cottesbrooke Hall in Northamptonshire, a Queen Anne mansion dating from 1702, which now houses the greatest collection of sporting and equestrian art outside the USA. Sculptures and paintings by artists such as George Stubbs, Ben Marshall and Alfred Munnings immortalize the horses and hounds of former owners. The collection was started at the end of the 19th century by Sir James Buchanan, later Lord Woolavington, after whom it is named.

There is no evidence that Jane Austen ever visited Northamptonshire, but at the time she was writing *Mansfield Park* she asked her sister, Cassandra, and her friend Martha Lloyd to provide details about the landscape of the county. In a letter to Cassandra dated 29 January 1813, Austen wrote, 'If you could discover whether Northamptonshire is a county of hedgerows, I should be glad.' In a letter to Martha the

Cottesbrooke Hall in Northamptonshire

following month, she wrote, 'I am obliged to you for your enquiries about Northamptonshire but do not wish to renew them, as I am sure of getting the intelligence I want from Henry, to whom I can apply at some convenient moment *sans peur et sans reproche*.'

Logan Pearsall Smith was among several Austen scholars who had no doubt that Cottesbrooke was the model for Mansfield Park. He visited the estate in 1935 and published his impressions the following year in *Reperusals and Recollections*. He points out that the name of the owners of Mansfield Park was Langham and that Cottesbroke Hall was built by a man called Sir John Langham. Describing his visit, he recalls seeing the stairs where the character of Edmund found the young Fanny in tears shortly after her arrival at Mansfield Park and the breakfast room where she wrote to her brother William. Then Pearsall Smith went into the library and billiard room, where the rehearsal for the group's play, *Lovers' Vows*, took place.

Pearsall Smith admits that he does not know whether Jane Austen ever went to Cottesbrooke Hall, but he says that there is good reason to believe that she was acquainted with the Sir James Langham of the time, and that her brother Henry was familiar with his family. Although Henry might have described the layout of the house to his sister, says Pearsall Smith, she conveys it so accurately in her novel that anyone making 'this most delightful of all Jane Austen pilgrimages' would find it hard to believe that she had not been to Cottesbrooke herself.

'A rogue…but a civil one'
John Murray publishes Emma

When Thomas Egerton refused to issue a second edition of *Mansfield Park*, Jane Austen decided to look elsewhere for a publisher. Through the agency of her brother Henry, the manuscript of *Emma* was offered to John Murray in Albemarle Street, Piccadilly. The proprietor of the firm at the time, John Murray II, was a leading

Lord Byron

publisher of travel and history books and poetry, notably Lord Byron, but had not previously published novels. His son John Murray III would later gain notoriety as the publisher of Charles Darwin's *On the Origin of Species*.

In November 1814, Murray's reader, William Gifford, wrote that he had 'nothing but good to say' about *Emma*, and Murray offered £450 for the copyrights of *Sense and Sensibility*, *Mansfield Park* and *Emma*. Acting as an unofficial go-between, Henry Austen pointed out that his sister had made more than that amount from 'one very moderate edition of *Mansfield Park* and a still smaller one of *Sense and Sensibility*'.

Murray eventually agreed to publish a first edition of *Emma* and a second edition of *Sense and Sensibility* on profit-sharing terms. Jane Austen said of her new publisher, 'He is a rogue of course, but a civil one.'

Although pleased to be published by Murray, Jane was exasperated by the slow production process, which resulted in the book not being available to the public until January 1816. Following the publication of *Emma*, all profits were offset against losses on a reprint of *Mansfield Park*, so Jane received only £38 18s. 1d. The cheque from Murray even spelt her name incorrectly, as Austin rather than Austen.

Emma and Miss Bates in Emma

Scott's adulatory review
The considerable impact of Emma

Jane Austen started writing *Emma* on 21 January 1814, saying, 'I am going to take a heroine whom no one but myself will much like.' In the event, this was not the case at all. Emma is likable, intelligent and well meaning – indeed, some readers prefer her to Austen's other leading female characters – but she is also conceited and over-confident. Having always had her own way in life, Emma has come to believe that she possesses a superior judgement that will allow her to influence the lives of others for their own good. The novel shows how this inflated self-belief leads the heroine astray, and how she fails to grasp the truth about other people's motives and feelings.

To some critics, including Jane Austen's biographer David Cecil, *Emma* represents the climax of Austen's literary career, but the author herself was worried about how the novel would be received. She admitted to being haunted by the idea that 'to those readers

Walter Scott

who have preferred *Pride and Prejudice* it will appear inferior in wit and to those who have preferred *Mansfield Park* inferior in good sense'. However, the Austen family were full of praise, and their enthusiasm was endorsed by a general readership when the novel was published in December 1815 (but dated 1816). The first edition consisted of 2,000 copies, of which 1,200 were sold in the first year.

Jane Austen's growing literary prominence was reflected by the inclusion in the March 1816 edition of the *Quarterly Review* of a long and highly complimentary article devoted to her work.

Although the piece was unsigned, it was known to have been written by the revered novelist Walter Scott, who identified *Emma* as representing a new class of fiction 'which draws the characters and incidents introduced more immediately from the current of ordinary life than was permitted by the former rules of the novel'.

Walter Scott's review delighted the author, even though she was annoyed that he had failed to mention *Mansfield Park* in his wide-ranging comments. Indeed, Scott's admiration for Austen increased with time. Ten years later he wrote in his diary:

Also read again, and for the third time at least, Miss Austen's very finely written novel of *Pride and Prejudice*. That young lady has a talent for describing the involvements and feelings and characters of ordinary life, which is to me the most wonderful I ever met with. The big Bow-Wow strain I can do myself like any now going; but the exquisite touch which renders ordinary

commonplace things and characters interesting from the truth of the description and the sentiment is denied to me.

'NO STORY IN IT'

Contemporary readers of **Emma** *were not universally impressed. Jane Austen sent a presentation copy to Maria Edgeworth, an author whose early Gothic novels had influenced her writing. Luckily, Austen did not have a chance to read Edgeworth's abrupt verdict on the book, revealed in a letter to her*

Maria Edgeworth

brother: 'There was no story in it, except that Miss Emma found that the man whom she designed for Harriet's lover was an admirer of her own – & he was affronted by being refused by Emma & Harriet wore the willow [grieved for the loss of a loved one].'

By royal permission
Emma *dedicated to the* Prince Regent

For the whole of Jane Austen's short life, the king of Great Britain was George III, who reigned – in name at least – for 60 years. As early as the 1780s, the king had shown signs of the debilitating illness that worsened as he grew older and would eventually lead him to be pronounced 'mad'. Thus on 6 February 1811 his eldest son, George Augustus Frederick, was sworn in as Prince Regent.

Although the Regency period, which lasted until George III's death in 1820, saw a great flowering of arts, architecture and culture in Britain, the Prince Regent himself was notorious for his extravagant and dissolute lifestyle, and his ill treatment of his wife, Princess Caroline of Brunswick. The playboy Prince Regent was an admirer of the novels of Jane Austen, but the author disapproved of his immoral behaviour and, when asked to dedicate *Emma* to him, was reluctant to do so.

The request had come about by a strange sequence of events. While staying in London to nurse her brother Henry through an illness, Jane met one of Henry's doctors, who was also physician to the Prince Regent and told her of the royal enthusiasm for her work. Jane was then invited to the Prince Regent's library at Carlton House, where the librarian, James Stanier Clarke, suggested that she might like to dedicate her next novel to his royal master.

At first, the response was negative. Jane's niece, Caroline Austen, recalled in her memoir that her aunt 'had no intention of accepting the honour offered – until she was avised [sic] by some of her friends that she must consider the

George Augustus Frederick, the Prince Regent

in Morocco leather with the Prince of Wales' feathers on the spine.

It did not take long for Austen followers to speculate that the dedication must have been written not by the author but by John Murray himself, who was clearly in no doubt where his best interests lay:

TO
HIS ROYAL HIGHNESS
THE PRINCE REGENT.
THIS WORK IS,
BY HIS ROYAL HIGHNESS'S
PERMISSION,
MOST RESPECTFULLY
DEDICATED,
BY HIS ROYAL HIGHNESS'S
DUTIFUL
AND OBEDIENT
HUMBLE SERVANT,
THE AUTHOR.

permission as a command'.

Having accepted defeat and conceded that the royal 'permission' was indeed a command, Jane proposed a simple dedication that read: *Emma, Dedicated by Permission to H.R.H. The Prince Regent*. However, when the novel was published in December 1815 by Jane Austen's new publisher, John Murray, it included a long and fulsome dedication to the royal patron, and the presentation copy was bound (at the author's expense)

BANKRUPT

*In March 1816, Austen, Maunde &
Tilson, the bank in which Henry
Austen was a partner, failed, and
Jane's favourite brother went
bankrupt, entailing losses to several
members of the family. Particularly
badly affected were his uncle James
Leigh Perrot, who lost £10,000,
and his brother, Edward Knight.
Henry decided that banking was
not the profession for him and
that, after all, he would do better
as a clergyman. A few months
later he took holy orders and was
soon appointed rector of Bentley in
Hampshire, a village between Alton
and Farnham, beginning a new
career as an evangelical preacher.
Three years later, following the
death of his brother James, Henry
temporarily assumed responsibility
for Steventon parish, until in 1823
his nephew William Knight was
ready to take charge.*

The duties of aunts
*Jane Austen advises on
literature and love*

While writing *Emma*, which
took less than a year to
complete, Jane Austen was busy
giving literary guidance to her
niece Anna Austen (later Lefroy),
who had set her heart on becoming
a novelist. 'You are now collecting
your people delightfully,' Jane wrote
to Anna on one occasion, 'getting
them exactly into such a spot as
is the delight of my life; 3 or 4
families in a country village is the
very thing to work on.'

In 1814 Anna had begun a novel
called *Enthusiasm*, later changed
to *Which is the Heroine?* When
each instalment was finished
she sent it off to her aunt, who
replied with detailed criticism and
advice. These letters reveal much
about Jane Austen's views on the
subject of her art. She advises
Anna not to write about people
and places of which she has no
direct knowledge, for example,
and to avoid the use of cliché, and
she emphasizes the importance

of making a story credible.

Jane Austen corresponded with another niece, Fanny Knight, on affairs of the heart. When Fanny expressed doubts about her love for a certain John Plumptre, Jane wrote, 'Oh! dear Fanny, your mistake has been one that thousands of women fall into. He was the first young man who attached himself to you. That was the charm, & most powerful it is.'

By February 1817, Fanny was involved in a new love affair, with James Wildman of Chilham Castle, near Godmersham in Kent. 'My dearest Fanny,' wrote Jane in response to her niece's request for an opinion, 'You are inimitable, irresistible. You are the delight of my life... You are the paragon of all that is silly & sensible, commonplace & eccentric, sad & lively, provoking and interesting... Oh! what a loss it will be when you are married.'

Although Jane insisted that Fanny should be in no hurry to marry, she had to acknowledge that, when it came to material advantages, wedlock was a lot more attractive than remaining unmarried. 'Single

women have a dreadful propensity for being poor,' she admitted.

Jane Austen took the duties of aunts very seriously. 'Now that you are become an aunt, you are a person of some consequence & must excite great interest whatever you do,' she wrote in October 1815 to another niece, Caroline Austen. Caroline was the half-sister of Anna Lefroy, who had just given birth to her first child. 'I have always maintained the importance of aunts as much as possible,' proclaimed Jane.

Caroline was another aspiring writer who sent her stories to Jane Austen for evaluation, and her brother Edward (Jane's future biographer), had started a novel, which his aunt had praised. When part of Edward's novel was mislaid, Jane wrote to him insisting that she had nothing to do with its disappearance and giving insight into her own creative method: 'What should I do with your strongly, manly, spirited sketches, full of variety and glow? How could I possibly join them on to the little bit (two inches wide) of ivory on which I work with so fine a brush, as produces little effect after much labour?'

As it turned out, none of the nephews and nieces of whom Jane Austen was particularly fond would become published novelists. Indeed, Anna Lefroy destroyed her novel after Jane's death, telling her daughter that she could not bear to go on with it because it reminded her so much of the loss of her aunt.

EARLY FOREIGN EDITIONS

The year of Emma*'s publication also saw the appearance in print of the first foreign translation of Jane Austen's works.* **Raison et Sensibilité, ou les Deux Manières d'Aimer** *appeared in France in 1815, followed in 1816 by* **Le Parc de Mansfield, ou Les Trois Cousines** *and* **La Nouvelle Emma, ou les Caractère Anglais du Siècle.** Emma *was also published in Philadelphia, USA, in 1816. A French translation of* **Persuasion** *published in 1822 appeared as* **La Famille Elliot.**

RAISON
ET
SENSIBILITÉ,
OU
LES DEUX MANIÈRES D'AIMER.
TRADUIT LIBREMENT DE L'ANGLAIS,
PAR
Mme ISABELLE DE MONTOLIEU.

TOME PREMIER.

À PARIS,
CHEZ ARTHUS-BERTRAND, LIBRAIRE,
RUE HAUTEFEUILLE, N°. 23.
1815.

Title page from the first French edition of Sense and Sensibility

The preference among publishers of the time to use personal names in book titles rather than abstract ideas goes back to the first American edition of **Pride and Prejudice,** *which appeared in 1832 as* **Miss Elizabeth Bennet.** *A. A. Milne, the author of books about Winnie the Pooh, used the same title for his 1936 dramatization of the novel.*

Cinderella revisited
Persuasion *divides opinion*

Jane Austen's last completed novel, *Persuasion*, was written at a time when the author had started to suffer the debilitating symptoms of Addison's disease (as we now know it), the affliction from which she is believed to have died. She finished the first version, which had taken about a year to write, on 18 July 1816, but she was not happy with it.

'She thought [the ending] tame and flat, and was desirous of producing something better,' according to her nephew Edward Austen-Leigh. 'This weighed upon her mind, the more so probably on account of her poor health, so one night she retired to rest in very low spirits.' The next morning she awoke feeling more

Anne Eliott and Captain Wentworth in Persuasion

positive and cheerful. She discarded the unsatisfactory chapter and wrote two more to replace it. 'The result is that we possess the visit of the Musgrove party to Bath; the crowded and animated scenes at the White Hart hotel,' wrote Austen-Leigh, 'and the charming conversation between Captain Harville and Anne Elliot, overheard by Captain Wentworth, by which the two faithful lovers were at last led to understand each other's feelings.'

Although the revised ending is generally considered an improvement on the original, the novel has continued to divide opinion. In *The Common Reader*, Virginia Woolf describes *Persuasion* as combining 'a peculiar beauty' with 'a peculiar dullness', suggesting that Austen may have become less interested in the kind of character traits and foibles that had once proved such a rich source of satire and comedy. Woolf also notices a loss of gentleness and subtlety in Austen's writing, and a fading sensitivity to the delights and diversions of everyday life.

Woolf detects a new element in *Persuasion*, however, which had prompted the philosopher William Whewell to describe it as 'the most beautiful of her works'. Indeed, Woolf believes that in the novel Jane Austen reveals a growing awareness of the mysterious and romantic possibilities of the big wide world, which she had so far known only slightly.

The novel has been characterized by others as a Cinderella story, featuring a heroine who is unappreciated and exploited by those around her, a handsome prince who is diverted by the charms of others, a moment of enlightenment, and the final happy ending. In Anne Elliot, Austen brings to life a character who, in the words of the narrator, 'had been forced into prudence in her youth [and] learned romance as she grew older – the natural sequence of an unnatural beginning'.

THE CHARMS OF OLDER WOMEN

'It is something for a woman to be assured, in her eight-and-twentieth year, that she has not

*lost one charm of earlier youth,'
reflects Anne Elliot near the end
of* **Persuasion,** *by which time she
has regained confidence in Captain
Wentworth's love.* **Persuasion**
*is the only one of Jane Austen's
novels to feature as the central
character a woman who, by the
standards of the time, is no longer
young. In this respect, the book
could be interpreted as an homage
to single older women – all those
who might seem to have lost
their chance of marriage, but for
whom there might still be some
hope of finding true happiness.*

In her sister's arms
Cassandra loses her beloved Jane

By the spring of 1817 it was
clear to Jane Austen that she
was seriously ill, although she
continued to put up a good front
to those around her. In April, after
several months of worsening health,
she made a will, leaving everything
to her sister Cassandra, apart from
£50 to her brother Henry and £50
to his housekeeper. Later she wrote

a note leaving a gold chain to her
goddaughter Louisa Knight and
a lock of her hair to her beloved
niece Fanny Knight.

When her local doctor admitted
bafflement at her symptoms, Jane
was advised to consult Giles King
Lyford, the eminent surgeon-in-
ordinary at the county hospital
in Winchester. On 24 May,
accompanied by Cassandra, Jane
set out on the 14-mile (22km)
journey, with her brother Henry
and William, the son of her brother
Edward, riding on each side of
the carriage.

Lodgings were found for Jane
and Cassandra at College Street,
a cul-de-sac close to Winchester
College, where Henry had been
to school. Although Jane seemed
to rally slightly after her arrival
in Winchester, in mid-July her
condition took a serious turn for
the worse. Informed by Dr Lyford,
James and Henry told Jane that she
had not long to live. She took the
news calmly but asked if she might
have the sacrament administered
to her while she was still able to
appreciate its significance. The

College Street in Winchester,
where Jane Austen died

ceremony was duly performed.

On the afternoon of 17 July, Cassandra, coming back from the town, found Jane in a weak state. It passed off slightly, but soon returned, along with severe pain, causing her to cry out, 'God, grant me patience. Pray for me, oh pray for me!' When asked what she wanted, Jane said that she wanted nothing but death. By 7.00pm she was unconscious, and at 4.30am on Friday 18 July she died in her sister's arms. She was 41 years old.

Jane was buried in Winchester Cathedral early on the morning of Thursday 24 July. Neither her mother nor her sister attended the service; it was less usual then for women to go to funerals. The extent of Cassandra's misery is evident in the letter she wrote to her niece Fanny after the funeral:

I watched the little mournful procession the length of the street; and when it turned from my sight, and I had lost her for ever, even then I was not overpowered, nor so much agitated as I am now in writing of it. Never was human being more sincerely mourned by those who attended her remains than was this dear creature.

LOVE STORY

The intimacy and tenderness of the love scene involving Anne Elliot and Captain Wentworth at the end of **Persuasion** *has led many readers to assume that Jane was telling a love story of her own – although even more readers have challenged this assertion. Among the former was the writer*

Rudyard Kipling

Rudyard Kipling, who in 1926 was prompted to compose a comical poem called 'Jane's Marriage'. This describes Jane ascending to heaven, where she is greeted by Shakespeare and other famous writers, as well as three archangels. The angels offer to grant her any wish; when she requests 'love', they search the universe for a man who loved her. He is found in Hampshire reading a book called Persuasion, which tells the story of the relationship between him and Jane. From there, the man (apparently Captain Wentworth) is taken into paradise to be reunited with her in heavenly 'marriage'.

Gothic parody
And Northanger's 'horrid' novels

Although it was the first of Jane Austen's novels to be completed (under the title *Susan*), *Northanger Abbey* was not published in its revised form until after the author's death, in a joint edition with *Persuasion*. Jane's brother Henry undertook the task of seeing the four-volume work through the press. Prefaced with a 'Biographical notice of the Author' by himself, the two novels appeared together in December 1817 (though dated 1818). The title *Northanger Abbey* was invented by Henry. The book is basically a parody of the Gothic fiction that was popular at the time, exemplified by Mrs Radcliffe's melodramatic novel *The Mysteries of Udolpho*, published in 1794.

The heroine of *Northanger Abbey*, Catherine Morland, makes a fool of herself by expecting life to be like the tales of romantic terror that are her favourite reading. Quite distinct from the serious comedy at the heart of *Sense and Sensibility*, the light-hearted humour of *Northanger*

Catherine Morland and Isabella Thorpe in Northanger Abbey

reveals Jane Austen at her most high-spirited and sparkling, yet the narrative never loses contact with an ironic sense of reality.

Several Gothic authors and novels are mentioned in the book, including Fanny Burney and *The Monk: A Romance* by Matthew Lewis. Catherine Morland is given by her friend Isabella Thorpe a list of seven books commonly referred to as the 'Northanger "horrid"

novels'. Initially thought to be Jane Austen's invention, they are now known to be real – all seven were republished in 1968 by The Folio Society:

Castle of Wolfenbach by
  Eliza Parsons
Clermont by
  Regina Maria Roche
*The Mysterious Warning,
  a German Tale* by Eliza Parsons
*The Necromancer, or the Tale
  of the Black Forest* by
  Ludwig Flammenberg
The Midnight Bell by
  Francis Lathom
The Orphan of the Rhine
  by Eleanor Sleath
Horrid Mysteries by
  the Marquis de Grosse

PERFECT SUMMARY
*In **Northanger Abbey**, Jane Austen praises the novels she admires most as displaying 'thorough knowledge of human nature, the happiest delineation of its varieties, the liveliest effusions of wit and humour,*

conveyed to the world in the best chosen language'. This summary perfectly encapsulates the qualities that Austen sought to reproduce in her own works of fiction.

Literary genius ignored
Winchester Cathedral's three memorials

Six days after her death in the summer of 1817, Jane Austen was buried in the north aisle of Winchester Cathedral. Today, the cathedral has not one but three memorials to her.

For more than 50 years, the only mark of remembrance was a simple stone slab. Its inscription, written by her favourite brother Henry, made much of her 'charity, devotion, faith and purity', but failed even to mention her achievements as a writer:

In memory of Jane Austen, youngest daughter of the late Revd. George Austen, formerly Rector of Steventon in this County. She departed this

life on the 18th of July 1817, aged 41, after a long illness supported with the patience and the hopes of a Christian.

The benevolence of her heart, the sweetness of her temperament, and the extraordinary endowments of her mind obtained the regard of

Brass tablet memorial at Winchester Cathedral

all who knew her and the warmest love of her intimate connections.

Their grief is in proportion to their affection. They know their loss to be irreparable but in their deepest affliction they are consoled by a firm though humble hope that her charity, devotion, faith and purity have rendered her soul acceptable in the sight of her Redeemer.

Eventually a second memorial was erected, again in the north aisle – a brass tablet paid for by the profits from Edward Austen-Leigh's 1870 memoir of his aunt and installed near her grave. The inscription refers in passing to her books, but Christian faith and piety again take centre stage:

Jane Austen, known to many by her writings, endeared to her family by the varied charms of her character and ennobled by Christian faith and piety was born at Steventon in the county of Hants Dec xvi mdcclxxv and buried in this cathedral xxiv mdcccxvii. She openeth her mouth with wisdom, and in her tongue is the law of kindness.

In 1898, money was raised by public subscription for a stained-glass window to be erected in the cathedral in addition to the two existing memorials. It was designed by Charles Eamer Kempe and set into the north wall directly above the brass tablet. The window includes a figure of St Augustine and a figure of King David playing his harp. Elsewhere St John holds an edition of his Gospel open at the first page: 'In the beginning was the Word…' There is a Latin inscription that translates as follows: 'Remember in the Lord Jane Austen who died July 18th A.D. 1817.' Four other figures in the window each carry scrolls with Latin inscriptions alluding to Jane's religious nature – but there is still no reference to her literary genius.

Novel fragment
The 'completion' of Sanditon

On 17 January 1817, despite worsening illness, Jane Austen had begun a new novel, which her family believed was to be called *The Brothers*. She laid down her pen on 18 March, after writing some 22,000 words – and would never take it up again for literary purposes.

Set against the background of a coastal town in the midst of development as a health resort, the novel fragment, which later became known as *Sanditon*, introduces the reader to more than 20 characters. It consists of a series of satirical portraits designed to ridicule the same kind of human traits that Jane Austen had mocked in her youth: affectation, melodrama, stupidity and sentimentality. Interestingly, given the author's physical state, it also makes fun of people who make too much fuss about their health.

Since Jane Austen stopped writing *Sanditon* two centuries ago, there have been numerous attempts to complete the novel. The first was made by Jane's niece Anna Lefroy, who did not finish it either. More recent examples have been prompted by the desire to know and tell what happened after the last sentence Austen wrote: 'Mr Hollis, poor Mr Hollis! It was impossible not to feel him hardly used: to be obliged to stand back in his own house and see the best place by the fire constantly occupied by Sir Henry Denham.' A selection of the more than 80 *Sanditon* 'completions' that have so far appeared includes:

Sanditon: Jane Austen's Unfinished Masterpiece Completed by Jane Austen and Juliette Shapiro

The Brothers by Jane Austen and Another Lady

Cure for All Diseases by Reginald Hill

Jane Austen's Charlotte: Her Fragment of a Last Novel completed by Julia Barrett

Sanditon: Jane Austen's Last Novel Completed by Jane Austen and Another Lady

The Suspicion at Sanditon (or *The
    Disappearance of Lady Denham*)
    by Carrie Bebris
A Return to Sanditon by
    Anne Toledo

FANNY'S BETRAYAL

*In 1820 Jane Austen's niece
Fanny Knight, 'the delight of [her
aunt's] life', married Sir Edward
Knatchbull, a baronet 18 years
her senior. It was a marriage that,
in Fanny's view, had elevated her
in the world – to the extent that
she would afterwards look back
with embarrassment and disdain
at her apparently obscure and
provincial Austen relations. It was
a sad irony that the niece that
Jane Austen had loved best showed
disloyalty in the end – and revealed
herself to be the type of character
that her aunt, during her literary
career, had so enjoyed to satirize.*

Early critics
'Too washy' or 'next to Shakespeare'?

Many critics have drawn attention to the influence of *Pride and Prejudice* on Elizabeth Gaskell's *North and South* (1855), whose main character, Margaret Hale, also has experiences that bear comparison to those of Fanny Price in *Mansfield Park*. However, Mrs Gaskell's evident admiration for her literary predecessor was not shared by all her literary contemporaries. The letter-writer Jane Carlyle described Jane Austen's work as 'too washy; water-gruel for mind and body at the same time [is] too bad', while the cleric John Henry Newman wrote in 1837, 'Miss Austen has no romance – none at all. What vile creatures her parsons are!'

Writing in 1834, Sara Coleridge, daughter of the poet Samuel Taylor Coleridge, remarked, 'My uncle Southey and my father had an equally high opinion of her merits, but Mr Wordsworth used to say that though he admitted that her novels were an admirable copy of life, he could not be interested in productions of that kind; unless the truth of nature were presented to him clarified, as it were, by the pervading light of imagination, it had scarce any attractions in his eyes.'

In the opinion of the novelist Charlotte Brontë: '[Austen's] business is not half so much with the human heart as with the human eyes, mouth, hands, and feet. What sees keenly, speaks aptly, moves flexibly, it suits her to study; but what throbs fast and full, though hidden, what the blood rushes through, what is the unseen seat of life and the sentient target of death – this Miss Austen ignores.'

In fact, little public interest was taken in Jane Austen's work between her death in 1817 and the publication of a memoir by her nephew Edward Austen-Leigh in 1870. Yet there was a small band of admirers who championed her writing from the start. The theologian and academic Richard Whateley, Archbishop of Dublin, writing in 1821, was the first to compare Austen to Shakespeare.

Alfred Lord Tennyson

This was a comparison taken up in 1843 by Thomas Babington Macaulay in respect of her powers of caricature, and in the 1850s by the literary critic George Henry Lewes, who, writing in *Blackwood's Magazine*, praised Austen's novels for 'the economy of art...the easy adaptation of means to ends, with no aid from superfluous elements'. Another who put Jane Austen 'next to Shakespeare' was Alfred Lord Tennyson, the poet laureate.

FAY WELDON'S LETTERS TO ALICE

In **Letters to Alice on first reading Jane Austen,** *published in 1984, the novelist Fay Weldon assumed the role of a fictional aunt to write a series of letters to her imaginary 18-year-old niece, Alice (see also Comic Spirit). Alice is expected to study Jane Austen at school, but she is not interested in her novels and cannot grasp why her writing is so much admired. Alice's 'aunt' tries to persuade her that she would be foolish not to make the effort to understand and appreciate what Austen was doing, especially since Alice herself is trying to write a novel. In this illuminating exploration of the art of creative writing, Weldon echoes a sequence of letters that Jane Austen actually did send to her niece Anna Austen (later Lefroy), who was trying to become a novelist, and which summed up Jane's views on what was important in life and in literature.*

'Highest esteem'
Genius celebrated in the American Republic

The earliest surviving accolade for Jane Austen's work to emanate from the USA appeared in a letter to her brother Francis, dated 6 January 1852. Written 35 years after the author's death, it came from the Quincey family of Boston, Mass., whose ancestor 'held a high rank among the first emigrants to New England' and who had several descendants who had distinguished themselves in public office.

'Since high critical authority has pronounced the delineations of character in the works of Jane Austen second only to those of Shakspeare [sic], transatlantic admiration appears superfluous,' wrote the correspondent, a Miss Quincey. 'Yet it may not be uninteresting to her family to receive an assurance that the influence of her genius is extensively recognized in the American Republic, even by the highest judicial authorities.' It transpired that Mr Chief Justice

Marshall of the US Supreme Court and his deputy Mr Justice Story held Jane Austen in the highest esteem as a writer. 'To them we owe our introduction to her society,' explained Miss Quincey. 'For many years her talents have brightened our daily path, and her name and those of her characters are familiar to us as "household words".'

Having obtained Sir Francis Austen's address from their friend Admiral Wormley, the Quinceys wanted to thank the Austens for 'the sentiments of gratitude and affection' that Jane had inspired. Their desire now was to receive more information about the novelist and perhaps even a memento. 'The autograph of his sister, or a few lines in her handwriting, would be placed among our chief treasures,' said Miss Quincey.

Sir Francis composed an appropriate reply and, by way of a gift, sent the Quinceys a long letter written by Jane.

IDOLATROUS LOVE

In the preface to an 1894 edition of **Pride and Prejudice,** *the literary scholar George Saintsbury coined the term 'Janeites' to describe the quality of idolatrous love that defined the growing band of Jane Austen fans. The term has since been both embraced by devotees of Austen's work and used to deride people who appear to appreciate*

George Saintsbury

Austen in the 'wrong' way. In 1924, Rudyard Kipling published a short story entitled 'The Janeites' about a group of World War I soldiers who were secretly fans of Austen novels. An epigraph at the start of this story is devoted to the memory of Jane Austen. It praises God for creating Austen and for all her works, and celebrates the memorial stones to the author located in Winchester Cathedral and Milsom Street, Bath.

Facts of life
Modern biographical interpretations

The facts of Jane Austen's life, such as they are known, are largely drawn from the detailed memoir of her nephew Edward Austen-Leigh, published in 1870 – parts of which have been dismissed by critics as a hagiography. Yet the paucity of information about the author has not prevented many writers in the two centuries since her death from attempting to tell the story of Jane Austen's life – by drawing on her writings and her letters, as well as personal memoirs by those who knew her. Her most respected biographers include Elizabeth Jenkins (*Jane Austen: A Biography*, 1938) and David Cecil (*A Portrait of Jane Austen*, 1978).

The Canadian writer Carol Shields is particularly interested in the use of satire in the author's early writings. In Shields' biography *Jane Austen*, she identifies a yearning to entertain, influence and to be acknowledged that remained the motivation for Jane Austen's writing throughout her life. Among the most eminent of Austen's biographers is the award-winning writer Claire Tomalin, who argues in *Jane Austen: A Life* that Austen's decision not to marry was a crucial factor in allowing her to achieve her literary potential.

In *The Real Jane Austen*, Paula Byrne overcomes the lack of biographical information by examining Austen's life and work through 18 objects connected with the author. Her interpretation of the artefacts is often unexpected. For example, topaz crosses, gifts to

Jane and her sister, Cassandra, from their seafaring brother Charles (see Gold Chains and Topaz Crosses), form the basis for a discussion about homosexuality in the navy, then punishable by death.

Other recent biographical works include:

Deirdre Le Faye, *Jane Austen: A Family Record*, Cambridge University Press, 2003

Janet Todd, *Jane Austen: Her Life, Her Times, Her Novels*, Andre Deutsch, 2013

John Mullan, *What Matters in Jane Austen? Twenty Crucial Puzzles Solved*, Bloomsbury, 2013

Claudia L. Johnson, *Jane Austen's Cults and Cultures*, University of Chicago Press, 2014

'Swell show'
Austen goes to Hollywood

In October 1935, the comedian Harpo Marx saw a play in Philadelphia that made a great impression on him. It was *Pride and Prejudice, a sentimental comedy in three acts* by an Australian playwright called Helen Jerome. The next day, Harpo sent a telegram to Irving Thalberg in Hollywood, saying that he had just seen a 'swell show' named *Pride and Prejudice*, and that it would be perfect for Norma. Thalberg was head of production for MGM and Norma was his wife, the actress Norma Shearer, who had recently been nominated for an Oscar for her portrayal of Elizabeth Barrett Browning in *The Barretts of Wimpole Street*. Harpo Marx had in mind for Norma the role of Elizabeth Bennet, and Norma was indeed attracted by the proposal.

MGM bought the rights to the play for US $50,000, and Clark Gable was among several leading actors lined up to take the role of Darcy. In the event, Thalberg died before the film could be made,

Harpo Marx

released in 1940, the reviews were generally excellent, with the *New York Times* critic describing it as 'deliciously pert'. The film also inspired a surge of popular interest in Jane Austen, with many new editions of her six novels appearing in print. Among these was a 25-cent paperback of *Pride and Prejudice* from Pocket Books in New York, which prefigured the boom in mass-market paperback publishing.

By the time the film came out, World War II had begun, but the USA had not yet joined it. According to Rachel Brownstein, author of *Why Jane Austen?*, it served an important propaganda purpose: the film aimed to entertain and educate American audiences, but also to encourage them to assist England, which was under attack from Germany.

but the project was kept alive and the search for actors continued. The choice for Darcy eventually fell on Laurence Olivier, who had already made a name for himself in *Wuthering Heights* and *Rebecca*. A leading candidate for Elizabeth Bennet was Vivien Leigh, who was having an affair with Olivier; she was turned down because of fears of a moral backlash if the affair became public, and Greer Garson was chosen instead.

When the film was finally

WORLDWIDE PHENOMENON

Writing in 1975 in **Jane Austen: Bicentenary Essays,** *Andrew Wright highlights the extraordinary appeal in non-English-speaking countries of Jane Austen's work, which – like that of Shakespeare – was, and remains, a worldwide phenomenon. Under the title 'Jane Austen Abroad', Wright records that, within the past 20 years,* **Pride and Prejudice** *had made its appearance, or reappearance, in Austria, Belgium, Brazil, China, Czechoslovakia, Egypt, Finland, France, Germany, Holland, Iceland, Italy, Japan, Mexico, Portugal, Romania, Spain, Sweden, Switzerland, Turkey, the USSR and Yugoslavia. Today, the American website Goucher holds translations of Jane Austen's works in more than 40 different languages. Such foreign translations involve not only the main western European languages, but also Afrikaans, Arabic, Farsi, Hebrew, Hindi, Mandarin Chinese, Swahili, Taiwanese and Urdu.*

Editor's hand
William Gifford adds perfect polish

Jane Austen is celebrated as a supreme literary stylist. However recent academic research has revealed that an editor working for the publisher John Murray may have been responsible for the perfectly polished sentences of her later fictional works.

After studying about 1,100 pages of the novelist's unpublished manuscripts, Professor Kathryn Sutherland of Oxford University has concluded that Jane Austen's style was far more free-flowing than it appears in the finished books. The manuscripts reveal Austen to be an experimental and innovative writer, constantly trying new things and even better at writing dialogue than the style of her published novels suggests. But the author's own manuscripts also feature blots, crossing outs and a way of writing described by Sutherland in an interview published on the BBC Entertainment and Arts website as 'counter-grammatical'.

Professor Sutherland argues that William Gifford, an associate of John Murray II, who started publishing Jane Austen's works in 1815, is likely to have been heavily involved in the editing process. Her research formed part of an initiative to create an online archive of all Austen's handwritten manuscripts, which is now available at Jane Austen's Fiction Manuscripts: www.janeausten.ac.uk.

Jack Russell terrier

DOG PLAYS DARCY AND TILNEY

Wishbone *is a children's TV show that was first broadcast on American PBS (Public Broadcasting Service) in the 1990s. It features a Jack Russell terrier named Wishbone who daydreams about starring in screen adaptations of classic books and is known as 'the little dog with the big imagination'. When Wishbone's young owner, Joe Talbot, becomes involved in incidents that recall well-known works of literature, Wishbone takes the lead in acting out the work in question,* usually in costume. He plays Mr Darcy in 'Furst Impressions', the **Wishbone** adaptation of **Pride and Prejudice**. Then in 'Pup Fiction', an adaptation of **Northanger Abbey**, he plays Henry Tilney, frightening Catherine Morland with an invented Gothic story and teaching her that taking books too seriously can get you into trouble.*

Cult status
*Modern-day Austen worship
in North America*

Two centuries after her death, Jane Austen has become a pop-culture phenomenon, the inspiration for numerous romantic films and chick-lit publications. Nowhere is this more apparent than on the North American continent, as indicated by the huge success of the Jane Austen Society of North America (JASNA).

Dedicated to the enjoyment and appreciation of Jane Austen and her writing, JASNA has more than 5,000 members and more than 75 regional groups in the USA and Canada. Apart from Alaska, Arkansas, North Dakota and West Virginia, every US state has at least one branch of the society. Its members, who are of all ages and from all walks of life, share an enjoyment of Jane Austen's fiction and the company of like-minded readers.

Jane Austen-style tea party

With their regular conventions, Regency costumes and self-written 'sequels' to the novels, Austen devotees display a fervour that has elevated their heroine to cult status. Some Janeites, as they call themselves, write their own fiction imagining the marital exploits of Mr and Mrs Darcy. Others put on elaborate period dress and throw tea parties and balls with a Jane Austen theme. Screen versions of Jane Austen's works, such as the 2005 film of *Pride and Prejudice* starring Keira Knightley as Elizabeth Bennet, contributed to a surge of interest in all things Austen. The Janeite subculture itself became the subject of a popular comic novel, Shannon Hale's *Austenland*. The film version of this novel had its premiere at the 2013 Sundance Film Festival in Utah, the largest independent film festival in the USA.

White gowns and bonnets
The indispensable items of Regency fashion

The enthusiasm for Jane Austen around the world is based not only on her novels and characters, but also on everything to do with the way of life of the author and her characters, including clothes, food and social customs. People attending the regular Austen festivals enjoy nothing more than dressing up in Regency clothing and attending the kind of balls that were held at the fictional Netherfield or Mansfield Park.

One distinctive fashion piece that occurs in Jane Austen's novels is the white gown. For example, Miss Tilney in *Northanger Abbey* always wears white, and we know from Austen's letters that she herself owned white dresses. Indeed, the simple white gown of her day could be compared with the black dress of today; it was a basic fashion item for every season that no stylish woman could be without.

in white. No, I see no finery about you; nothing but what is perfectly proper.'

Another indispensable fashion item of the time was the bonnet, which came in all shapes and sizes, made of lace, linen or muslin and trimmed with ribbon. In her novels and letters, Jane Austen frequently mentioned trimming new hats and redecorating old bonnets as a female activity.

Today there are numerous websites and blogs that explain how to recreate the fashions of Jane Austen's time, as well as illuminating other aspects of Regency life. Among the most prominent of these are:

Jane Austen's World
janeaustensworld.wordpress.com

Jane Austen Centre
www.janeausten.co.uk

Republic of Pemberley
pemberley.com

Women wearing typical Regency clothing and bonnets

For centuries, white had signified purity and chastity, and simple white cotton dresses were associated with an idealized view of pastoral life. When Fanny Price in *Mansfield Park* worries that she is overdressed for a dinner party in a white gown made for her to wear to her cousin's wedding, she is told by Edmund Bertram, her future husband, 'A woman can never be too fine while she is all

Desert Island books
Austen selections on radio show

The popular BBC radio show *Desert Island Discs* interviews prominent 'castaways' (one each week) and asks them to choose eight pieces of music, one book – in addition to Shakespeare and the Bible or an equivalent religious text – and one luxury item that they would choose to take with them to an imaginary desert island.

Since 1974, 20 guests on the show have named works by Jane Austen as their book choice. The most popular single novel has been *Pride and Prejudice*, followed by *Emma*, but several people opted for *The Collected Works*. *Sense and Sensibility*, *Mansfield Park* and *Persuasion* have gained one vote each, but no one chose *Northanger Abbey*. Here is the list of Austen fans with their book choices and the date on which the interview with them was first broadcast on *Desert Island Discs*:

Bruce Tulloh:
Long-distance runner
Pride and Prejudice
23 November 1974

Duncan Grant:
Painter and designer
The Collected Works
15 March 1975

Sir Oliver Millar:
Surveyor of the Queen's Pictures
Emma
4 June 1977

Dame Daphne du Maurier:
Author and playwright
The Collected Works
3 September 1977

Angela Rippon:
TV broadcaster
Pride and Prejudice
16 January 1982

Dame Janet Baker:
Opera singer – mezzo-soprano
Persuasion
7 August 1982

Charlotte Lamb:
Romantic novelist
Pride and Prejudice
10 September 1983

Maureen Lipman:
Actor, writer and comedian
The Collected Works
19 January 1986

Robert Armstrong, Baron Armstrong of Ilminster:
Civil servant
The Collected Works
24 July 1988

Jeffrey Tate:
Conductor
The Collected Works
12 February 1989

Kathleen Turner:
Hollywood film star
Emma
14 May 2000

Marguerite Patten:
Food writer and broadcaster
Pride and Prejudice
21 January 2001

Theresa May

Dame Kristin Scott Thomas: Actor
Sense and Sensibility
30 March 2003

Graham Norton:
Comedian and broadcaster
Mansfield Park
2 May 2004

Jack Mapanje:
Writer and poet
Pride and Prejudice
24 October 2004

Karren Brady, Baroness Brady:
Sports executive, TV personality
and author
Pride and Prejudice
30 December 2007

Dame Heather Rabbatts:
Lawyer, businesswoman
and broadcaster
Pride and Prejudice
24 July 2011

Dame Carolyn McCall:
Chief executive, Easyjet
Pride and Prejudice
6 October 2013

Professor Tanya Byron:
Clinical psychologist
and TV presenter
Emma
27 Oct 2013

Rt Hon. Theresa May MP:
Politician who, in July 2016,
became the UK's second woman
Prime Minister
Pride and Prejudice
23 November 2014

CHURCHILL'S TONIC

In 1942, during World War II, the British Prime Minister Winston Churchill fell seriously ill with pneumonia and was confined to bed for several weeks. His doctors insisted that he should not work, so, in order to pass the time, he resorted to reading novels. Churchill wrote in his memoirs that, remembering that he had read **Sense and Sensibility** *in the past, and enjoyed it greatly, he had*

Winston Churchill

therefore chosen **Pride and Prejudice.** *He found it a marvellous tonic to immerse himself in the calm and seductive social milieu created by Jane Austen, which was seemingly unaffected by tumultuous contemporary events such as the French Revolution and the Napoleonic Wars. The main interest in the novel, he decided, was to see to what extent natural passions could be controlled by mores and manners. He also enjoyed Austen's exposition of the plot, consisting of plausible and well-reasoned explanations of the misfortunes that had befallen her characters.*

Darcymania
Serial becomes a cultural phenomenon

Since its first screening in 1995, the scene in the BBC TV adaptation of *Pride and Prejudice* in which Mr Darcy goes swimming in his lake at Pemberley – and emerges dripping wet to greet his future bride, Elizabeth Bennet – has been viewed on YouTube more than 4.7 million times, and the figure continues to rise. Adapted by Andrew Davies, the serial starring Colin Firth as Darcy and Jennifer Ehle as Elizabeth has become a cultural phenomenon; it is one of the BBC's most popular TV serials ever made. In Britain, the final episode had a market share of 40 per cent of TV viewers, and the entire first run of VHS videos sold out within two hours of release. Ehle and Firth were widely praised for their performances, with Firth's lake scene regarded as one of the most unforgettable moments in British TV history.

Even before its brooding hero took the plunge in episode

four, *Pride and Prejudice* was a sensation. Ten million viewers were captivated by it; newspaper columns – most notably Helen Fielding's 'Bridget Jones's Diary', at that time a regular item in the *Independent* newspaper before it became a successful book and film – were stricken by 'Darcymania'. A Bollywood-style *Bride and Prejudice* by Gurinder Chadha followed in 2004, and Keira Knightley played Elizabeth Bennet in Joe Wright's film dramatization in 2005. But however many Austen adaptations there were on the big and small screens, it was the 1995 BBC TV version that they tried to imitate.

Professor Deborah Cartmell of DeMontford University in Leicester, the author of *Jane Austen's Pride and Prejudice: The Relationship Between Text and Screen*, believes that the lake scene – which was added by Davies – has almost usurped the original novel in the minds of the public. She points out that, since the serial was first broadcast, every cultural reference to Jane Austen, and every adaptation, has had as much to do with Andrew Davies

as with Jane Austen. ITV's 2008 series *Lost in Austen* and a 2013 film, *Austenland*, both centre on *Pride and Prejudice* fans – but the Mr Darcy they dream about is the damp one played by Colin Firth.

Zombie mash-up
A new interpretation of Pride and Prejudice

Literary–horror 'mash-ups' are a new phenomenon in the book-publishing market, with Seth Grahame-Smith's *Pride and Prejudice and Zombies* leading the way. Published in the spring of 2009, the book became an instant bestseller, with more than 700,000 copies sold in the first few months. The idea was the brainchild of Jason Rekulak, an editor at Quirk Books in Philadelphia, who compiled a list of classic works of literature that might benefit from an influx of pop-culture figures such as pirates, ninjas and zombies. He approached Seth Grahame-Smith, a TV writer, with the proposal to link *Pride and Prejudice* with zombies – and the rest is history.

Regency zombie

are so instantly recognizable that they lend themselves well to absurd juxtapositions. Also in 2009, Quirk Books published *Sense and Sensibility and Sea Monsters* by Ben H. Winters.

A film version of *Pride and Prejudice and Zombies* was released in 2016, with Lily James playing Elizabeth. 'Liz Bennet is already just the coolest, most independent and wonderful character,' says James. 'Give her a sword and she gets even better.'

Gripping continuation
Jane Austen meets P. D. James

The thrust of the plot is as follows. With 19th-century England threatened by a plague of the undead, the five Bennet sisters are reinvented as skilled martial arts warriors, while Fitzwilliam Darcy is a renowned monster-hunter with superior Japanese fighting skills. The wide appeal of *Pride and Prejudice and Zombies* seems to be based primarily on the comedy of incongruity, which depends on familiarity with the original. Jane Austen's characters

P. D. James, one of the queens of crime fiction, combines her meticulous plotting with Jane Austen's sharp-eyed characterization in a gripping continuation of *Pride and Prejudice* called *Death Comes to Pemberley*, published in 2011. The book begins six years after the marriages of both Elizabeth Bennet and her elder sister, Jane, to Fitzwilliam Darcy and Charles Bingley respectively, while preparations are under way at the

Darcy residence, Pemberley, for the annual autumn ball.

The evening before the ball, the hosts and their guests are enjoying an informal family dinner followed by music. They are preparing to retire for the night when Darcy sees from the window a chaise being driven at speed down the road from the direction of the wild woodlands. When the horses are pulled up, Lydia Wickham, Elizabeth's youngest sister, almost falls from the carriage, hysterically screaming that her husband has been murdered.

Darcy organizes a search party and, with the discovery of a blood-smeared corpse in the woodlands, the peace of both the Darcys and of Pemberley is shattered as the family becomes involved in a criminal investigation. Eventually, the body of Wickham's great friend, Captain Denny, is discovered with horrible injuries and Wickham is charged with his murder.

The BBC's three-episode dramatization of *Death Comes to Pemberley*, screened in the UK during December 2013, was a high point of Christmas TV viewing.

Critics generally praised this dramatization for its plot, and its 'sumptuous' appearance.

P. D. James

AMATEUR SLEUTH

Francine Mathews, an American writer of mystery and spy fiction, is the author of a series of historical novels that feature the character of Jane Austen as an amateur sleuth. Her Austen novels are written under the pseudonym of Stephanie Barron, and presented as entries in journals recently 'discovered' in the basement of an old house that was previously owned by one of Jane's relatives. There have been 13 books published in the series so far:

Jane and the Unpleasantness at Scargrave Manor *(1996)*

Jane and the Man of the Cloth *(1997)*

Jane and the Wandering Eye *(1998)*

Jane and the Genius of the Place *(1999)*

Jane and the Stillroom Maid *(2000)*

Jane and the Prisoner of Wool House *(2001)*

Jane and the Ghosts of Netley *(2003)*

Jane and His Lordship's Legacy *(2005)*

Jane and the Barque of Frailty *(2006)*

Jane and the Madness of Lord Byron *(2010)*

Jane and the Canterbury Tale *(2011)*

Jane and the Twelve Days of Christmas *(2014)*

Jane and the Waterloo Map *(2016)*

Sparking a Twitterstorm
Bank governor yields to protests

Proposals in 2013 to make Jane Austen the new face of the UK's £10 bank note ignited an inferno of rape and death threats from Twitter users. The feminist campaigner Caroline Criado-Perez received around 50 abusive tweets an hour for a 12-hour period after she successfully campaigned for Austen to appear on the note. Her campaign attracted more than 35,000 signatures after the Bank of England revealed that it was planning to replace prison reformer

Jane Austen silhouette

truly deserving of the accolade of appearing on a bank note, since she was widely acknowledged as one of the greatest writers in the history of English literature.

Not everyone is pleased about the image of Jane Austen that has been chosen to appear on the note. However Elizabeth Proudman, chair of the Jane Austen Society, pointed out that the image reflected the only authentic image of Jane in existence, drawn by her sister, Cassandra, in the late 18th century (see Solitary Sketch). Her nephew Edward Austen-Leigh commissioned an engraving of the author (based on Cassandra's drawing), which was said by relatives to be a fair likeness.

Elizabeth Fry with wartime leader Winston Churchill on new £5 notes – meaning there would be no woman other than the Queen on sterling bank notes.

At a press conference at Chawton cottage on 24 July 2013, the Bank of England governor, Mark Carney, confirmed that – following the high-profile campaign – Jane Austen would appear from 2017 on the £10 note, which will be printed on polymer. He said that Jane Austen was

NOTE FEATURES

The reverse of the Jane Austen £10 note (see Sparking a Twitterstorm) will include:

- *A quotation from* **Pride and Prejudice***: 'I declare after all there is no enjoyment like reading!' (Caroline Bingley).*
- *A portrait of Jane Austen commissioned by her nephew Edward Austen-Leigh in 1870, adapted from an original sketch by her sister, Cassandra.*
- *An illustration of Elizabeth Bennet undertaking 'the examination of all the letters which Jane [Bennet] had written to her' from a drawing by Isabel Bishop.*
- *An image of Godmersham Park, the home of Edward Knight, Jane Austen's brother, which is believed to feature in some of her novels.*
- *An image of the 12-sided writing table and writing quills used by the author at Chawton cottage.*

Social implications
Jane Austen and food

Meals are rarely discussed in detail in Jane Austen novels but, when they are, there are always social implications. In *Pride and Prejudice* Mrs Bennet invites a group of guests, including Mr Bingley and Mr Darcy, to a family dinner where it is obvious that her main priority is to impress. She wrote afterwards to her daughter Jane, who had been present at the occasion:

> The dinner was as well dressed as any I ever saw. The venison was roasted to a turn – and everybody said they never saw so fat a haunch. The soup was fifty times better than what we had at the Lucases' last week; and even Mr Darcy acknowledged, that the partridges were remarkably well done; and I suppose he has two or three French cooks at least.

Jane Austen's evident interest in food has prompted numerous cookery writers to produce blogs and books on an Austen theme.

Recently published titles include:

Kim Wilson, *Tea with Jane Austen*,
   Frances Lincoln, 2011
Pen Vogler, *Dinner with Mr Darcy*,
   Cico Books, 2013
Maggie Lane, *Jane Austen and Food*,
   Endeavour Press, 2015
Pen Vogler, *Tea with Jane Austen*,
   Cico Books, 2016

The language of food

However, the really dedicated cook in the Austen household was Jane and Cassandra's friend, Martha Lloyd, who lived with the sisters and their mother for many years at Chawton cottage. Martha's recipes were collected in *A Jane Austen Household Book* by Peggy Hickman (David and Charles, 1977) and in *The Jane Austen Cookbook* by Maggie Black and Deirdre Le Faye (British Museum Press, 1995). As a taster, here is Martha's recipe for Swiss Soup Meagre:

Take four cabbage lettuces, and endive, sorrel, spinach, cherville, chives, onions, parsley, beet leaves, cucumber sliced, peas and asparagus; let all these herbs be cut fine and no stalks be put in. Then put a quart of a pound of butter in a stewpan, shake over your herbs when they are in the butter a small teaspoonful of flour and let them stew some time then pour in a quart of boiling water and let it stew on till near dinner time, then add the yolks of three eggs in a teacup of cream. Broth is better than so much water if you have it. If you have not all the vegetables above mentioned it will be very good with what you have or a little Seville orange juice if you like. Salt and peper [sic] to taste.

JANE AUSTEN WAXWORK

A life-size waxwork of Jane Austen is a new attraction at the Jane Austen Centre in Bath. Based on a 2002 portrait by Melissa Dring, the waxwork figure was created by portrait sculptor Mark Richards. During the three years that it took to complete the sculpture, Richards collaborated closely with Melissa Dring and with Nell Clarke, a hair and colour artist who used to work at Madame Tussaud's. Award-winning designer Andrea Galer dressed the completed figure in authentic period costume. Located in a former Georgian townhouse, the Jane Austen Centre tells the story of the author's time in Bath, where she lived for five years, from 1801 to 1806.

Manly men
Male protagonists on screen

Few people know Jane Austen's works better than Andrew Davies, who wrote the screenplay for the six-part TV serial of *Pride and Prejudice* (1995), the TV films of *Emma* (1996) and *Northanger Abbey* (2007), and the three-part TV serial of *Sense and Sensibility* (2008). He also wrote the scripts for the two Bridget Jones films that were inspired by Austen's work, *Bridget Jones's Diary* (2001) and *Bridget Jones: The Edge of Reason* (2004).

A particular challenge for Davies in all his Austen adaptations has been how to represent the male protagonists in true manly fashion. Jane Austen's self-imposed rule never to write a scene without a woman in it prompted him to introduce episodes that were not in the original books, so that audiences could appreciate the male characters in the round. These scenes generally show men engaged in traditionally masculine pursuits, such as hunting, shooting and galloping over the hills on horseback, so viewers can see

Edward Ferrars in Sense and Sensibility

that they have a life apart from making polite conversation in drawing rooms.

In *Sense and Sensibility*, Davies wrote a log-splitting scene for Edward Ferrars, in which the character – throwing off his jacket and picking up an axe – uses the activity of splitting logs to relieve his feelings about being trapped in an unwanted engagement. For Colonel Brandon he wrote a falconry scene, in which a hawk swoops down and comes to rest on his wrist. In a symbolic yoking of power with gentleness, Brandon sensuously strokes the falcon's feathers – just at the moment when

Marianne Dashwood is coming across the field to see him.

AUSTEN-THEMED BOOKS

A never-ending stream of books based on the themes of Jane Austen's novels continues to roll off the presses, covering everything from husband-hunting to vampires. Here is a recent list of such publications compiled by the leading American bookseller Barnes and Noble:

Austenland *by Shannon Hale (2007) – an original story.*

Longbourn *by Jo Baker (2013) – an original story based on* **Pride and Prejudice.**

Emma *by Alexander McCall Smith (2015) – a modern retelling of* **Emma.**

Eligible *by Curtis Sittenfeld (2016) – a modern retelling of* **Pride and Prejudice.**

Pride and Prejudice and Zombies *(2016) by Seth Grahame-Smith – a modern reinterpretation of* **Pride and Prejudice.**

Spotlight on Cincinnati
The fourth addition to the Austen Project

In 2016, the American novelist Curtis Sittenfeld hit the literary headlines with a modern retelling of *Pride and Prejudice* located in her hometown of Cincinnati, Ohio. This is the fourth book in the Austen Project series, in which six bestselling modern authors are paired with Jane Austen's six complete works: Joanna Trollope has produced a new version of *Sense and Sensibility*; Val McDermid takes on *Northanger Abbey*; and Alexander McCall Smith gives his own interpretation of *Emma*.

Sittenfeld's new book turns the spotlight on Cincinnati's upper middle class, among whom is Elizabeth Bennet, a magazine journalist who has wasted years with a married man, and Mr Darcy, a haughty neurosurgeon. Long before his arrival in Cincinnati, everyone knows that Charles Bingley, known as Chip, is looking for a wife – for Chip had appeared two years earlier on the fictional TV dating show, *Eligible*.

Sittenfeld has identified similarities between an early 19th-century English village (Jane Austen's Meryton) and a medium-sized Midwestern city in modern USA (Cincinnati). Even though such places may seem dull and uninteresting to outsiders, she says, people who live there see them as full of drama and intrigue.

Cincinnati skyline

In the novel *Eligible*, Elizabeth Bennet's first encounter with Darcy and Bingley takes place at a barbecue, where she overhears the two men talking about her. To her huge indignation, when Chip remarks that she is single, Darcy replies that he's 'not surprised'. He then mocks the people of Cincinnati in general, and notes that they are obsessed with matchmaking.

Despite his rudeness and arrogance, Darcy exudes sexual energy from the moment that he appears in *Eligible*, enhanced by his high-status job as a neurosurgeon. Elizabeth Bennet, meanwhile, is a journalist who has a lot more autonomy than the Lizzie of Jane Austen's world. Sittenfeld's characters are inspired by Austen's characters but they have their own separate identities.

The author argues that, to make the plot work, the threat of looming financial crisis must hang over the Bennets. She shows that it is Mr Bennet's failure to take out medical insurance that brings financial disaster on his family, but what interests her most is where the Bennets fit into the social structure. They are rich by most people's standards, but compared with the super-rich they could be regarded as struggling to survive.

Sittenfeld gives us a new interpretation of what she sees as the central theme in all Austen's novels: the subtle interaction between people of various social classes and how they manage (or not) to resolve their differences.

NEED OF A HUSBAND

Jane Austen's posthumously published novel **Lady Susan** *was brought to the screen in 2016 for the first time by American writer–director Whit Stillman under the name* **Love and Friendship,** *the title of a quite separate piece of Austen juvenilia. Kate Beckinsale plays Lady Susan, a beautiful widow with no financial means who is in need of a husband. Reginald De Courcy, the man on whom she sets her sights, is played by Xavier Samuel, and her scheming American confidante, Mrs Johnson, by Chloë Sevigny.*

Literary legacy
Six books that changed the world

In total Jane Austen completed six novels, all of which were published during her lifetime or in the year after her death. In order of publication, they are as follows:

Sense and Sensibility (1811)
Jane Austen started writing the novel in 1795, when she was 19, but it was not until 1811 that it was published on commission, which meant that the author had to pay for the production costs. Her brother Henry acted as intermediary in negotiations with the publisher, Thomas Egerton. Conceived as a novel-in-letters entitled *Elinor and Marianne*, it was recast two years later as a third-person narrative and renamed *Sense and Sensibility*. A second edition appeared in 1813.

Pride and Prejudice (1813)
Begun in the autumn of 1796, and initially entitled *First Impressions*, the novel was published in January 1813 by Egerton. He paid £110 for the copyright, a price generated by the success of its predecessor, *Sense and Sensibility*.

Mansfield Park (1814)
Jane Austen probably began writing the novel in 1811–12 and finished it in 1813. It was offered to Egerton that year and published in May 1814 in three volumes. After Egerton refused to reprint, a second edition was published by John Murray in 1816.

Emma (1815)
The novel was written between January 1814 and March 1815. Like *Sense and Sensibility*, it was published on commission, but this time by John Murray. It appeared in December 1815 (dated 1816 on the title page). At the request of the Carlton House librarian, the novel was dedicated to the Prince Regent.

Northanger Abbey (1818)
Generally regarded as the third of Jane Austen's novels, this did not appear in print until six months after the author's death. Austen finished the manuscript, which she

called *Susan*, in 1799. It was sold to Benjamin Crosby for £10 in 1803, but by 1809 no book had appeared. Despite complaints, the author did not recover the copyright until 1816. Renamed *Northanger Abbey*, the novel was eventually published by John Murray in a joint first edition with *Persuasion*.

Persuasion (1818)

Begun in the summer of 1815, the novel was finished in the summer of 1816, by which time the author had started to succumb to the illness that eventually killed her. She thought that the original ending was 'tame and flat' and rewrote it. *Persuasion* was published in a four-volume edition with *Northanger Abbey* by John Murray in December 1817 (1818 on the title page), together with a 'Biographical Notice of the Author' by Jane's brother Henry.

OTHER WORKS

*Besides her six completed novels (see Literary Legacy), other works by Jane Austen include her two unfinished novels, **The Watsons** and **Sanditon** (unpublished in her lifetime). She began **The Watsons** in 1803, abandoning it in 1805; then she was forced to stop writing **Sanditon** four months before her death because of worsening health. Austen also made a three-volume collection of her juvenile works, written in notebooks between 1787 (when she was 12) and 1793, under the titles **Volume the First**, **Volume the Second** and **Volume the Third**. The original works survive – one in the Bodleian Library, Oxford, and the other two in the British Museum. **Volume the Second** includes both **Love and Freindship** [sic], an exuberant parody of the cult of 'sensibility', and the author's own version of **The History of England**. Finally, Jane Austen also wrote poems, prayers, a play called **Sir Charles Grandison** (adapted from a novel by Samuel Richardson) and a cornucopia of letters.*

Screen legacy
Austen film and TV adaptations

Since the first television adaptation of a Jane Austen novel appeared in 1938, followed in 1940 by the first cinema film, starring Greer Garson and Laurence Olivier in MGM's *Pride and Prejudice*, there have been more than 50 screen adaptations in the English language alone inspired wholly or partly by Austen's fiction, in addition to many radio and TV documentaries. Two centuries after Austen's death in 1817, there is no sign of a slackening in cinematic interest, with British actor Charlotte Rampling due to star in the first-ever screen dramatization of Austen's unfinished novel, *Sanditon*. Here is a list of the English screen adaptations to date:

Pride and Prejudice (1938)
BBC TV film written by Michael Barry, starring Curigwen Lewis and Andrew Osborn.

Pride and Prejudice (1940)
MGM film adaptation directed by Robert Z. Leonard and produced

by Hunt Stromberg, with screenplay by Aldous Huxley and Jane Murfin. The film starred Greer Garson and Laurence Olivier.

Emma (1948)
BBC TV film directed by Michael Barry and written by Judy Campbell, starring Judy Campbell and Ralph Michael.

Pride and Prejudice (1952)
Six-part BBC TV serial directed by Campbell Logan and written by Cedric Wallis, starring Daphne Slater and Peter Cushing.

Pride and Prejudice (1958)
Six-part BBC TV serial written by Cedric Wallis, starring Jane Downs and Alan Badel.

Emma (1960)
Six-part BBC TV serial directed by Campbell Logan and written by Vincent Tilsley, starring Diana Fairfax and Paul Daneman.

Persuasion (1960)
Four-part BBC TV serial directed by Campbell Logan, written by

Barbara Burnham and Michael Voysey, starring Daphne Slater and Paul Daneman.

Pride and Prejudice (1967)
Six-part BBC TV serial directed by Joan Craft and written by Nemone Lethbridge, starring Celia Bannerman and Lewis Fiander.

Sense and Sensibility (1971)
Four-part BBC TV serial directed by David Giles, with screenplay by Denis Constanduros, starring Joanna David, Ciaran Madden, Robin Ellis, Richard Owens and Patricia Routledge.

Persuasion (1971)
Five-part Granada TV serial directed and produced by Howard Baker, with screenplay by Julian Mitchell, starring Ann Firbank and Bryan Marshall.

Emma (1972)
Six-part BBC TV serial directed by John Glenister and produced by Martin Lisemore, with screenplay by Denis Constanduros, starring Doran Godwin and John Carson.

Pride and Prejudice (1980)
Five-part BBC TV serial adapted by Fay Weldon, directed by Cyril Coke and produced by Jonathan Powell, starring Elizabeth Garvie and David Rintoul.

Jane Austen in Manhattan (1980)
Merchant Ivory film made for the British TV company LWT, but later released for cinema viewing, in which rival film companies compete to produce their own versions of *Sir Charles Grandison*, a play that Jane Austen wrote in her childhood. Directed by James Ivory and produced by Ismail Merchant, with screenplay by Ruth Prawer Jhabvala, starring Anne Baxter, Robert Powell, Michael Wager and Sean Young.

Sense and Sensibility (1981)
Seven-part BBC TV serial dramatized by Alexander Baron and directed by Rodney Bennett, starring Irene Richard, Tracey Childs, Bosco Hogan and Robert Swann.

Mansfield Park (1983)
Six-part BBC TV serial directed
by David Giles and produced by
Betty Willingale, with screenplay by
Kenneth Taylor, starring Sylvestra
le Touzel and Nicholas Farrell.
The first screen adaptation of
Mansfield Park.

Northanger Abbey (1986)
BBC TV in association with
Arts & Entertainment Network.
A TV film directed by Giles
Foster and produced by Louis Marks,
with screenplay by Maggie Wadey,
starring Katharine Schlesinger, Peter
Firth and Robert Hardy.

Metropolitan (1990)
Written, directed and produced by
Whit Stillman. A loose adaptation
of *Mansfield Park*, set in New York.

Ruby in Paradise (1993)
Homage to *Northanger Abbey*
written and directed by Victor
Nuñez, starring Ashley Judd and
Todd Field.

Sense and Sensibility (1995)
Columbia Pictures film directed by
Ang Lee and produced by Lindsay
Doran, with screenplay by Emma
Thompson (see Star-studded).

Pride and Prejudice (1995)
Six-part BBC TV serial directed by
Simon Langton and produced by
Sue Birtwistle, with screenplay by
Andrew Davies, starring Jennifer
Ehle, Colin Firth, Alison Steadman
and Crispin Bonham-Carter.

Clueless (1995)
A coming-of-age comedy loosely
based on *Emma*, written and directed
by Amy Heckerling and produced by
Robert Lawrence and Scott Rudin,
starring Alicia Silverstone.

Persuasion (1995)
BBC Films/Sony Pictures film
directed by Roger Michell,
produced by Margot Hayhoe, with
screenplay by Nick Dear, starring
Amanda Root, Ciarán Hinds, Susan
Fleetwood and Corin Redgrave.

Emma (1996)
Film adaptation made for ITV, starring
Kate Beckinsale, Samantha Morton,
Samantha Bond and Mark Strong.

Directed by Diarmuid Lawrence and produced by Sue Birtwistle, with screenplay by Andrew Davies.

Emma (1996)

Miramax film starring Gwyneth Paltrow, Jeremy Northam, Alan Cumming, Toni Collette and Ewan McGregor. Written and directed by Douglas McGrath, and produced by Patrick Cassavetti and Steven Haft.

Clueless (1996–99)

An American TV sitcom based on the 1995 film of the same name (and loosely on *Emma*), created by Amy Heckerling and starring Rachel Blanchard, Stacey Dash and David Lascher.

You've Got Mail (1998)

Romantic comedy film written, directed and produced by Nora Ephron and starring Tom Hanks and Meg Ryan. Two people in an online romance don't know that they are also business rivals. The plot and characters were influenced by *Pride and Prejudice*.

Wishbone: 'Furst Impressions' and 'Pup Fiction' (1990s)

Children's TV show broadcast on American PBS in the 1990s, featuring a Jack Russell terrier named Wishbone who takes on roles based on characters in literature, including Mr Darcy and Henry Tilney.

Mansfield Park (1999)

Miramax and BBC Films co-production. Written and directed by Patricia Rozema and produced by Sarah Curtis, starring Frances O'Connor, Jonny Lee Miller and James Purefoy. The life of Jane Austen is incorporated into the film, as well as the issues of slavery and plantation life in the West Indies.

Bridget Jones's Diary (2001)

Romantic comedy directed by Sharon Maguire, with screenplay by Andrew Davies, Richard Curtis and Helen Fielding, starring Renée Zellweger, Hugh Grant and Colin Firth. Based on Helen Fielding's novel of the same name, written as an homage to *Pride and Prejudice*.

Pride and Prejudice: A Latter-Day Comedy (2003)
Modern adaptation set among Mormons in Provo, Utah, directed by Andrew Black, with screenplay by Anne Black, Jason Faller and Katherine Swigert.

Bride and Prejudice (2004)
Bollywood-style dramatization of *Pride and Prejudice* directed by Gurinder Chadha, with screenplay by Paul Mayeda Berges and Gurinder Chadha. Filmed in English with some Hindi and Punjabi dialogue.

Bridget Jones: The Edge of Reason (2004)
The novel by Helen Fielding, a sequel to *Bridget Jones's Diary*, is an homage to *Persuasion*, but the story was changed significantly for the film.

Pride & Prejudice (2005)
StudioCanal/Working Title film directed by Joe Wright, with screenplay by Deborah Moggach, starring Keira Knightley, Matthew Macfadyen, Brenda Blethyn and Donald Sutherland.

The Lake House (2006)
Remake of the Korean film *Il Mare* (2000), *The Lake House* is a time-travel story directed by Alejandro Agresti and starring Sandra Bullock, Keanu Reeves and Christopher Plummer. References to *Persuasion* feature prominently.

Material Girls (2006)
A modern-day teen comedy film about two rich and spoilt Hollywood socialites who suffer economic misfortune, based on the plot of *Sense and Sensibility*. Directed by Martha Coolidge with a script by John Quaintance, it stars Hilary and Haylie Duff, Anjelica Huston and Lukas Haas.

Mansfield Park (2007)
Granada TV co-production with WGBH/Boston. Directed by Iain B. MacDonald and produced by Suzan Harrison, with screenplay by Maggie Wadey, starring Billie Piper, Michelle Ryan and Blake Ritson.

Northanger Abbey (2007)
Granada TV co-production with

WGBH/Boston. Directed by Jon Jones and produced by Keith Thompson, with screenplay by Andrew Davies, starring Felicity Jones, JJ Field and Carey Mulligan.

Persuasion (2007)
Granada TV co-production with WGBH/Boston. Directed by Adrian Shergold, produced by David Snodin, with screenplay by Simon Burke, starring Sally Hawkins and Rupert Penry-Jones.

The Jane Austen Book Club (2007)
Romantic drama adapted from the 2004 novel of the same name by Karen Joy Fowler, focusing on a book club formed to discuss Austen's novels. Written and directed by Robin Swicord.

Becoming Jane (2007)
Biographical film based on Jane Austen's love for Tom Lefroy. Directed by Julian Jarrold with screenplay by Kevin Hood and Sarah Williams, starring Anne Hathaway, James McAvoy, Julie Walters, James Cromwell and Maggie Smith.

Twilight (2008)
Vampire romance film based on the novel of the same name by Stephenie Meyer, who drew on events and characters in *Pride and Prejudice*. Directed by Catherine Hardwicke, with screenplay by Melissa Rosenberg.

Sense and Sensibility (2008)
BBC Drama co-production with WGBH/Boston. Produced by Anne Pivcevic and directed by John Alexander, with screenplay by Andrew Davies, starring Hattie Morahan, Charity Wakefield, Janet McTeer, David Morrissey and Dominic Cooper.

Lost in Austen (2008)
Four-part Granada TV series written by Guy Andrews as a fantasy adaptation of *Pride and Prejudice*. Directed by Dan Zeff, it stars Jemima Rooper, Alex Kingston, Hugh Bonneville and Morven Christie.

Miss Austen Regrets (2008)
BBC Drama co-production
with WGBH/Boston based
on letters from Jane Austen to
her sister, Cassandra, and her
niece Fanny. Directed by Jeremy
Lovering and produced by Anne
Pivcevic, with screenplay by
Gwyneth Hughes, starring Olivia
Williams, Imogen Poots, Greta
Scacchi and Hugh Bonneville.

Emma (2009)
Four-part BBC TV drama serial
starring Romola Garai, Jonny
Lee Miller and Michael Gambon.
Directed by Jim O'Hanlon and
produced by George Ormond, with
screenplay by Sandy Welch.

Scents and Sensibility (2011)
Produced and directed by Brian
Brough, with screenplay by Brittany
Wiscombe and Jennifer Jan.

From Prada to Nada (2011)
Latino version of *Sense and
Sensibility*, in which two spoilt
sisters who have been left penniless
after their father's sudden death
are forced to move in with their
estranged aunt in Los Angeles.
Directed by Angel Gracia.

The Lizzie Bennet Diaries
(2012–13)
YouTube adaptation of *Pride and
Prejudice*, created by Bernie Su and
Hank Green of Pemberley Digital,
in which Lizzie Bennet (Ashley
Clements), a graduate student,
explains her life through the video
blog format.

Welcome to Sanditon (2013)
YouTube adaptation of Jane
Austen's unfinished novel *Sanditon*,
created by Bernie Su and Hank
Green of Pemberley Digital, and
starring Allison Paige.

Death Comes to Pemberley (2013)
Three-part BBC drama serial based
on the P. D. James novel of the
same name – a murder mystery
continuation of *Pride and Prejudice*.
Directed by Daniel Percival, with
screenplay by P. D. James and Juliette
Towhidi, starring Anna Maxwell
Martin and Matthew Rhys.

Austenland (2013)
Romantic comedy based on Shannon Hale's 2007 novel of the same name. Directed by Jerusha Hess and produced by Stephenie Meyer, it stars Keri Russell, JJ Field, Jane Seymour, Bret McKenzie and Jennifer Coolidge.

Emma Approved (2014)
Pemberley Digital multi-platform adaptation of *Emma*, created by Bernie Su and Hank Green.

Elinor and Marianne Take Barton (2015)
Updated online adaptation of *Sense and Sensibility*, directed by Oliver Cole and produced by Emily Rose.

Pride and Prejudice and Zombies (2016)
British–American comedy horror film based on the 2009 novel of the same name by Seth Grahame-Smith, which parodies Jane Austen's original work. Written and directed by Burr Steers.

Unleashing Mr Darcy (2016)
Romantic comedy that begins at a New York dog show. Directed by David Winning with screenplay by Teena Booth.

Love and Friendship (2016)
Romantic comedy based on Jane Austen's epistolary novel *Lady Susan*, but named after a piece of Austen juvenilia. Written and directed by Whit Stillman, it stars Kate Beckinsale, Chloë Sevigny, Xavier Samuel and Stephen Fry.

And here are a few foreign-language examples:

Crouching Tiger, Hidden Dragon (2000)
Director Ang Lee describes this Taiwanese–Chinese–American co-production as '*Sense and Sensibility* with martial arts'. With dialogue in Mandarin Chinese, it is the highest grossing foreign-language film in US history and has won more than 40 awards.

**Kandukondain Kandukondain
(I Have Found It! I Have
Found It!)** (2000)
Indian Tamil romantic film,
an adaptation of *Sense and
Sensibility*, directed and co-
written by Rajiv Menon.

Aisha (2010)
Hindi-language romantic comedy
directed by Rajshree Ojha and
starring Sonam Kapoor and
Abhay Deol. An adaptation of

Emma and based on the film
Clueless (1995), it is set in the
upper-class society of Delhi.

**Kumkum Bhagya (Marriage's
Luck)** (2014)
Hindi-language Indian TV soap
opera loosely based on *Sense and
Sensibility*, which follows the life
of a Punjabi matriarch, Sarla Arora,
who runs a marriage hall. Directed
by Sharad Pandey, and produced
and developed by Ekta Kapoor.

The Bennet family in Pride and Prejudice

STAR-STUDDED

The most star-studded film adaptation of Jane Austen's work ever made was probably the 1995 version of Sense and Sensibility *by Columbia Pictures. It was directed by Ang Lee, with screenplay by Emma Thompson, who also played Elinor Dashwood. The stately-home locations used for this film include Montacute House near Yeovil in Somerset and Saltram House near Plympton in Devon. The main cast of characters is as follows:*

Saltram House in 1832.

Elinor Dashwood –
  Emma Thompson
Marianne Dashwood –
  Kate Winslet
Edward Ferrars – Hugh Grant
Colonel Brandon –
  Alan Rickman
John Willoughby – Greg Wise
Mrs Dashwood – Gemma Jones
Mr Dashwood – Tom Wilkinson
John Dashwood – James Fleet
Sir John Middleton –
  Robert Hardy

Fanny Dashwood –
  Harriet Walter
Mr Palmer – Hugh Laurie
Mrs Jennings – Elizabeth Spriggs
Charlotte Palmer –
  Imelda Staunton
Lucy Steele – Imogen Stubbs
Margaret Dashwood –
  Emilie François

FURTHER READING

Since Jane Austen's death in 1817, numerous books and articles have been written about her life and works, and the times in which she lived. In recent years, the literary scope has widened to include Austen-themed blogs and websites, some associated with museums such as the Jane Austen Centre in Bath and the Jane Austen's House Museum in Chawton, Hampshire. Here is a representative selection of publications and online sources, including those consulted in the preparation of this book.

Books

J. E. Austen-Leigh, *A Memoir of Jane Austen and Other Family Recollections*, edited by Kathryn Sutherland, Oxford University Press, 2008.

Maggie Black and Deirdre Le Faye, *The Jane Austen Cookbook,* British Museum Press, 1995.

Rachel Brownstein, *Why Jane Austen?*, Columbia University Press, 2013.

Paula Byrne, *The Real Jane Austen*, William Collins, 2014.

Deborah Cartmell, *Jane Austen's Pride and Prejudice: The Relationship Between Text and Screen*, Bloomsbury, 2010.

David Cecil, *A Portrait of Jane Austen*, Penguin, 1980.

Sarah Jane Downing, *Fashion in the Time of Jane Austen*, Shire Library, 2010.

Seth Grahame-Smith, *Pride and Prejudice and Zombies*, Quirk, 2009.

Shannon Hall, *Austenland*, Bloomsbury, 2007.

Peggy Hickman, *A Jane Austen Household Book*, David & Charles, 1977.

Elizabeth Jenkins, *Jane Austen: A Biography*, Victor Gollancz, 1938.

Claudia L. Johnson, *Jane Austen's Cults and Cultures*, University of Chicago Press, 2014.

Maggie Lane, *Jane Austen and Food*, Hambleden Press, 1995.

Mary Lascelles, *Jane Austen and Her Art*, A & C Black, 1939.

Marghanita Laski, *Jane Austen and Her World*, Thames and Hudson, 1969.

Deirdre Le Faye, *Jane Austen: A Family Record*, Cambridge University Press, 2003.

Deirdre Le Faye, *Jane Austen's Letters*, Oxford University Press, 2014.

John Mullan, *What Matters in Jane Austen? Twenty Crucial Puzzles Solved*, Bloomsbury, 2013.

Laurel Ann Nattress, *Jane Austen Made Me Do It*, Ballantyne, 2011.

Carol Shields, *Jane Austen*, Weidenfeld & Nicholson, 2003.

John Sutherland and Deirdre Le Faye, *So You Think You Know Jane Austen? A Literary Quizbook*, Oxford University Press, 2009.

Richard Tanner, *Steventon, Jane Austen's Birthplace*, Greenhouse Graphics, 2008.

Janet Todd, *Jane Austen, Her Life, Her Times, Her Novels*, Andre Deutsch, 2013.

Claire Tomalin, *Jane Austen: A Life*, Penguin, 2012.

Pen Vogler, *Dinner with Mr Darcy*, Cico Books, 2013.

Pen Vogler, *Tea with Jane Austen*, Cico Books, 2016.

Fay Weldon, *Letters to Alice on First Reading Jane Austen*, Michael Joseph, 1984.

Kim Wilson, *Tea with Jane Austen*, Frances Lincoln, 2011.

Blogs and websites

Austenprose
austenprose.com

A blog devoted to Jane Austen's life and legacy. Includes more than 800 reviews of books, film and TV adaptations and merchandise related to 'Austenesque' fiction as well as to Jane Austen's own works and letters.

Chawton House Library
www.chawtonhouse.org

A research and learning centre for the study of early women's writing from 1600 to 1830, open to scholars and the general public alike. It is located in the manor house that once belonged to Jane Austen's brother, Edward Knight (formerly Edward Austen). The website includes biographies of an array of women writers, a blog, a podcast and a calendar of events.

Jane Austen Centre
www.janeausten.co.uk

Based in Bath, the Jane Austen Centre includes a permanent exhibition that explores Jane Austen's time in Bath and the influence of the city on her books, characters and personal life. The website has information about the annual Jane Austen festival, and an online magazine with sections on Austen's works, videos and reviews, and various aspects of Regency life: crafts and games, fashion and customs, recipes and dining.

Jane Austen's House Museum
www.jane-austens-house-museum.org.uk

Chawton cottage, where Jane Austen spent the last eight years of her life, is now the Jane Austen's House Museum. The website gives details of special exhibitions and events at the museum, and includes a blog covering a wide range of Austen subjects.

Jane Austen Society
www.janeaustensoci.freeuk.com

A UK-based organization that holds regular Austen-related events and publishes a biannual newsletter. The website has sections on publications, events and talks, biography, costume and social history.

Jane Austen Society of North America
www.jasna.org

A membership organization devoted to the appreciation of Jane Austen and her writing. The website includes information about news and events, activities of regional groups, book reviews, an annual essay contest, details of Austen screen adaptations and Austen-related merchandise.

Jane Austen's Fiction Manuscripts Digital Edition
www.janeausten.ac.uk

The digital 'reunification' of some 1,100 pages of fiction written in Jane Austen's own hand, complete with commentary and analysis. These manuscripts trace Austen's development as a writer from childhood to the year of her death (1787–1817).

Jane Austen's World
janeaustensworld. wordpress.com

A US blog that brings alive Jane Austen, her novels and the Regency period through food, dress, social customs and other historical details. It includes numerous links to sites and resources about British life and customs in the 18th and 19th centuries.

Masterpiece PBS
www.pbs.org/wgbh/ masterpiece/austen/

A section of the Masterpiece website, produced by American PBS (Public Broadcasting Service) is devoted to screen adaptations of Jane Austen novels. Includes interviews with actors and screenwriters, educational resources and a slideshow of interiors at Chawton cottage.

Republic of Pemberley
pemberley.com

A website based on discussion boards and themed Jane Austen pages, covering information about her characters and the locations of her novels. It includes digital text of Austen's novels and letters.

INDEX

OTHER GREAT TITLES FROM RYDON PUBLISHING

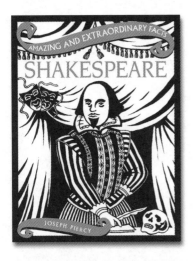

Amazing and Extraordinary
Facts: Shakespeare
Joseph Piercy
ISBN: 978-1-910821-06-0

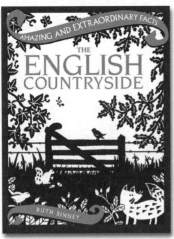

Amazing and Extraordinary
Facts: The English Countryside
Ruth Binney
ISBN: 978-1-910821-01-5

Plant Lore and Legend
Ruth Binney
ISBN: 978-1-910821-10-7

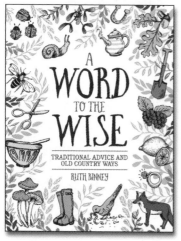

A Word to the Wise
Ruth Binney
ISBN: 978-1-910821-11-4

For more great books visit our website at **www.rydonpublishing.co.uk**

THE AUTHOR

Henrietta Heald is a writer and editor with a particular interest in British history, literature and the countryside. Her biography of the great Victorian inventor and industrialist William Armstrong, *Magician of the North*, was shortlisted for two literary prizes. She was chief editor of *Chronicle of Britain and Ireland* and *Reader's Digest Illustrated Guide to Britain's Coast*. Henrietta has also written two books on interior style: *La Vie est Belle* and *Coastal Living*. She has a degree in English Literature from Durham University and has long been fascinated by the works of Jane Austen.

AUTHOR ACKNOWLEDGEMENTS

Henrietta Heald would like to thank Richard Tanner, historian of Steventon in Hampshire and author of *Steventon – Jane Austen's Birthplace*, for his help with research for this book, which included an excellent guided tour of the village. The staff at Jane Austen's House Museum at Chawton were extremely helpful and informative. Henrietta would also like to thank Robert Ertle and Freya Dangerfield at Rydon Publishing for their support and words of wisdom, and Linda MacFadyen, friend and publicist, for her verve and vision.

PICTURE CREDITS